U R
A CREATOR

Design & Live

SAIBABU GORLA

BLUEROSE PUBLISHERS
India | U.K.

Copyright © Saibabu Gorla 2024

All rights reserved by author. No part of this publication may be reproduced, stored in a retrieval system or transmitted in any form or by any means, electronic, mechanical, photocopying, recording or otherwise, without the prior permission of the author. Although every precaution has been taken to verify the accuracy of the information contained herein, the publisher assumes no responsibility for any errors or omissions. No liability is assumed for damages that may result from the use of information contained within.

BlueRose Publishers takes no responsibility for any damages, losses, or liabilities that may arise from the use or misuse of the information, products, or services provided in this publication.

For permissions requests or inquiries regarding this publication, please contact:

BLUEROSE PUBLISHERS
www.BlueRoseONE.com
info@bluerosepublishers.com
+91 8882 898 898
+4407342408967

ISBN: 978-93-5989-806-3

Cover design: Muskan Sachdeva
Typesetting: Pooja Sharma

First Edition: January 2024

Dedicated

To

My Mother

A Guiding Force, Who Merged With Universe When I Was A Few Months Baby. Never Knew How She Looked Like As I Didn't Have A Single Picture Of Her.

Acknowledgements

With the deepest gratitude, I wish to thank my masters, my parents, my family and every person who has come and impacted my life through their presence.

I am thankful to the people who believed me and supported me in producing this book. My gratitude to the following people for their magnificent support.

Anil Kumar Turaga: For the unconditional affection, wisdom and guidance you bestowed upon my family and me over the last 28 years. You have been profoundly encouraging and helping me in completing this book. Thank you.

Vanaja Banagiri: This all started with your belief in my work. Thank you for your guidance and advice for making it happen.

Anuradha Evani: Thank you for all that you do mostly unseen. Your efforts made this book and its mission to help the people understand "They are the creators".

My daughter-in-law, Dr Bhavya Gorla: Who became my daughter. Thank you for your love, and for the deep joy you bring me every day. Thank you for your support.

My wife, Sailaja Gorla: I am truly blessed to have you in my life. Thank you for your incredible love and support like a mother.

How To Use This Book

I recommend you to read this book chapter wise and complete action steps before proceeding to the next chapter.

Otherwise, If you are committed to yourself for working on action steps, only then, read all the way once and complete the action steps mentioned at the end of each chapter.

Each topic with practice enables you to reach your goals and live the life on your own terms.

Make sure you have familiarised yourself with each of the topics; if required, read this book as many times as necessary.

This is your personal workbook - always keep it with you until you master it.

Step-By-Step Action Guide

To help you in setting your goals, action steps, relevant affirmations, visualisations and for scheduling, you can use the **uracreator** mobile app. You can download it in App Store or Play store.

You can reach me at: saibabug@uracreator.com

It's Your Life

You Create Your Own Reality

Close your eyes and say to yourself

"I Decide How I Want to Live"

Explore.........

Contents

My Experiment   xv

Who Am I   xix

1. The Physical Body   1
2. The Mind   7
3. Self-Talk   19
4. Core Values   39
5. Understanding Success   44
6. The Dream About Your Life   48
7. Setting Your Goals   56
8. Your Commitment   76
9. Developing Habits   84
10. The Power of Affirmations   97
11. The Power of Visualisation   107
12. Consistent-Persistence   117
13. The Power of Scheduling   122
14. The Art of Giving   129
15. Gratitude   133
16. Living with Non-Attachment   141

17. Living in the Present Moment	148
18. Meditation	154
19. The Importance of Yoga	163
20. You Are Perfect	177
21. Living Daily	182
Universe Expects Me to Live Like	*185*
References and Further Reading	*191*

My Experiment

If you hold this book with a determination to read it through and put what you learn into practice, it signifies that the universe is aligning to assist you in manifesting a joyful life. Embrace this opportunity.

Unusually since the age of 32, I had been in search of self-realisation. I started focusing on spiritual practices like reading self-help books, meditating deeply to keep my thoughts always positive. These practices profoundly impacted my thought patterns and changed my life.

My deep preoccupation in worldly affairs did not dilute my focus on spiritual practices even minutely.

Suddenly, something magical happened. I was 38 then.

I had a strange experience in which I felt as if my inner energy from the spine had left my head and been replaced by the energy from the outside. I experienced the feeling that what is inside the body is the same as what is outside. No difference at all. The experiential feeling of oneness occurred. I was in a blissful state for a long duration.

The universe confirmed with evidence that "What is inside of me is also outside of me." I experienced the oneness so intensely; that I started seeing myself in every living creature. In the moon, sun, plants, animals, insects and the entire cosmos. I could recognise myself in everything and everywhere.

For about 40 days, life was going on in a completely blissful state of mind. I questioned myself in my inner heart whether worldly affairs were needed? My inner voice questioned, "Who desired this life ?"

The instant reply was-"I desired everything, I came here as per my wish, I can't run away from my life, get back to your work and live with this experiential spiritual knowledge". With attention on my inner being, I received direct advice from the universe.

Nothing changed. In reality, I had undergone an internal change of thought and realised the truth that the outside world is a reflection of my own thoughts.

After realisation I felt, I should experience the effects of my earlier negative actions if any, so that I could be free from the cycle of Actions→Results→Actions→Results. This was my thought process. Immediately that's what manifested itself in my reality.

I am grateful for the magical realisation. Which allowed me, not to be concerned and did not allow me to deviate from my core values, even though I sold my house, office, cars, organisations and personal assets due to the global recession and local political circumstances.

I stopped setting goals for myself. When there were no goals, there were no specific results. Life was moving on its own. After a few years on this journey, I realised that, one should have heart-felt goals; and should not be attached to the outcome of the goals. But one should have goals. This is a must. The goals should help us to keep our awareness as per our wish. Otherwise, we will be carried away by the outside circumstances. I understood this, I changed my way of thinking and set goals for myself. Everything was back-business, new house, office, luxury cars, new projects.

What had changed? My own thoughts were the cause of my suffering as well as the cause of reviving my businesses. My own thoughts were responsible for my ascent descent and ascent again. I attracted negative experiences because I invited them. Later I realised this was the biggest misunderstanding.

Once you accept you are the universe, everything changes. Even your past actions won't have an impact on you; if you realise that you are infinite energy. We are atoms. How can energy have a past and a future? It is a well-known scientific law that Energy can neither be created nor destroyed. The energy is eternal and we are eternal.

Always remember that the universe is working through you and working for you too.

Our thoughts have the power to make or break us! I am a living example. I understood that humans are creating their lives through their own thoughts. The knowledge gained by reading different books and practices helped me to revive my thoughts and my life. Now I am living my life as per my wish.

The Universe inspired and propelled me to write this book to share the tools which helped me to create the life I am living now. I am enjoying every moment of my life, with no complaints. I am here with sharing the tools I made use of, I wish everyone make use of these for a joyful life.

Read, study, understand and practice the tools mentioned in this book to realise your true potential.

Don't expect to master any of the tools by the end of reading this book, rather expect to get a good and solid understanding of how these tools work, and the practical techniques for applying them in every aspect of your life.

It is your consistency in applying these tools in the coming months that will determine how much you actually benefit from them.

If you are consistent enough in your application, you will find your mental patterns and your habit patterns start changing gradually and you will be able to create a different lifestyle for yourself.

Once you identify your heartfelt priorities, these priorities will drive what you should focus on. Your life is lived very intentionally and purposefully. You make the right choices each day based on your priorities, you choose with whom you should spend time, and on what you spend your time.

The goal of this book is to help you understand who you truly are, and what potential you have, find your priorities, create and live as per your expectations.

Who Am I ?

The question seems to be simple. But are you truly aware of who you are? Most people are clueless. You must start by asking yourself, "Who am I ?" Anyone who asks such a question is likely to respond more about their profession than anything else. For instance, I am a doctor, or I am a student, or I am a homemaker, or I am a writer, and so on. If you're none of them, does it imply that you're nobody? No. In actuality, no matter what you do, where you live, how much money you have, or your social standing, we are all the same. In fact, it is the truth. We all share the same planet and the same essence. Surprised? So, let's simplify it. You can sum up your existence as pure energy. Everything in you—body, mind, and spirit—is made of energy. By understanding the physical body and the mind you will understand that you are nothing but energy.

1
The Physical Body

The human body having an average weight of 70kgs has about 37 trillion (37000 billion) cells and there are the same number of atoms in each cell. Scientifically your physical body is nothing but atoms. Do you ever feel that you are made up of so many atoms and that too with an incredible movement? You are habituated to the feeling that your body is solid, stable and quiet. This solidity is an illusion created by the brain but in fact, every moment trillions of chemical reactions are taking place in the body.

Every minute new cells are created when you eat, when you drink, and when you breathe. The human body excretes around 350 million dead cells each day in the form of sweat, urine, and other bodily wastes.

Atoms can neither be created nor destroyed. They can only be transformed. Your body's atoms are constantly being replaced at varying rates; some last for a few hours, some for months, some for years, but over the course of approximately 7 years, the majority will have been changed and you don't have the same body after 7 years.

Your body is made up of atoms that were previously found in the air, plants, animals, and minerals. Every atom in your body has a history. Since there are so many atoms involved, it's possible that some of the atoms in your body now, were once in the body of a well-known historical person or maybe your favourite movie star. The atoms in the food you eat, and the water you drink were once inside another human being.

Everyone, everything, You and I are nothing but atoms. No matter where you are or what you are doing; everyone is interconnected. And the entire universe is interconnected.

Atoms that are present in space are also present in your body. That means atoms are nothing but space. Space is infinite and you are also infinite; because you are also made out of this space. The body becomes invisible if it is seen with a high-powered microscope, which is nothing but universe!

The atoms in your body are merging with the Universe regularly. The physical body is in synergy with the external world at the level of atoms. At a fundamental level, all human beings in the past, present and future are equal; having the same infinite energy.

We human beings are atoms, which means that the universe is acting through this body. You need to understand what it wants to express through your body. This expression varies from person to person. This expression can only be identified by you, by going deep inside and starting to recognise the experiences which the universe wants to express through you.

Don't underestimate yourself. Be conscious that you are an energy being and have full potential, whatever you really wish to accomplish is attainable by you, because you have the infinite energy within you, like any other successful people.

You can activate the energy through your thoughts. It is through thinking you are doing all your worldly actions. What differentiates you from others is your thinking.

My Experiment

- By understanding that I am infinite energy the way I am operating my life has changed. Fear of losing anything is gone, even death.
- Started respecting every human being irrespective of their social status.
- Respecting my life partner, her views and treating her as an equal.
- Started treating my children as energy beings and supporting them as a guardian rather than imposing my ideas on them.
- Hurting other living beings means hurting my own self.
- Understanding the outcomes of my actions from others-point of view helps me in taking the right decisions.

Insight

- You are infinite energy.
- The universe is operating through you.
- All are interconnected and equal at the source level.
- Continuous energy exchange is happening in the body.
- You are forever in the form of atoms.
- The energy inside you, plants, animals and non-living things is the same.
- You are nothing but space.
- You have a superpower within you.

Action steps

(Read first and then practise)

- Close your eyes.
- Deeply inhale & slowly exhale three times to bring balance to your breath.
- Bring your thumb, forefinger and middle finger together of both hands separately and place them on your thighs and keep your spine straight.
- Now inhale, hold your breath without any thoughts as long as you are comfortable, now exhale.
- Repeat this three times.
- See yourself as a radiating sun or as energy in a lightning bolt.
- Now feel your entire body being filled up with radiating white light.
- With your inner eye; feel your family members also as energy bodies.
- Deeply inhale and feel the energy in each cell of your body.

Say to yourself –

- I am the universe and everyone is the universe.
- All my family members are energy.
- I have all the powers to manifest and create the life I wish.

- Open your eyes, rub your palms, feel the energy and place your palms on your face and absorb the energy into you.

Exercise:

- Whoever you come across feel them as energy. Internally say to yourself –We are equal.

2
The Mind

You don't see the mind with your gross eyes, only with the help of your consciousness you can watch your thoughts. You can see the thoughts in space. So you can define the mind as a vast space. Where your energy is focused in this space is called Awareness. Awareness moves; the mind does not.

When your awareness shifts to a certain area of the mind, you begin to experience that area of the mind. You will be aware of it as long as your awareness remains in this part of the mind. You are pure awareness travelling through different parts of the mind, not the mind. You have the ability to pick which part of your mind to focus on.

If you place your awareness in the happy area of the mind you will experience happiness. If you shift your awareness to the area of the mind where sadness is located, you will experience sadness. You can move your awareness from the sad area of the mind to any area of the mind you wish to go, by using your will-power.

Your awareness can travel within the mind and have different types of experiences. But it can only experience one area of the mind at a time. In the angry area of mind, you start experiencing anger. You are not angry, you are pure awareness, having an angry experience. Similarly, during a happy experience, you are pure awareness travelling within the mind. You can choose which area of the mind you wish to stay in.

Most individuals give up control of their decision-making process to people and things around them in exchange for permission to shift their awareness from one part of the mind to another during the day. People and things in their life take on the role of directors in their everyday lives. They are enslaved by everyone and everything around them.

You don't have to live like this. You have the ability to control your awareness and direct where you want it in your mind. You acquire freedom and control over your experience when you do this. Nobody can decide how you feel after you take control of your awareness unless you give them permission.

Everything in the universe is made up of energy and is vibrating at a certain frequency. There is no such thing as good or bad energy; there is just energy, vibrating at frequencies that are aligned with us or not. Certain frequencies uplift someone and drain others.

Your life is a manifestation of where you invest your energy. Where awareness goes; energy flows. Awareness is nothing but concentrated energy. As you focus your awareness, you focus your energy. As you withdraw your awareness, you withdraw your energy. And whichever area of the mind you go to, that is what you experience.

Wherever your awareness is in the mind, that is what you become conscious of.

Controlling where your consciousness travels gives you influence over what occurs in your life. The incapacity to harness and focus consciousness is mostly responsible for manifesting failure. You have control over where your awareness moves in your mind. Everything appears in the mind before appearing on the actual level. Manifestation begins with where your awareness is continually going.

Your awareness is governed by two forces. You are the first. The second factor is the people and things around you. You have acquired conscious mastery of awareness in the mind when you can direct where your awareness should go in your mind. You just need to make up your mind from this day onwards, and use your willpower and the power of concentration to guide where your awareness goes in your mind.

Concentration:

Concentration is the ability to keep awareness on one thing until you consciously choose to move it on to something else. When you are doing any particular task you completely focus on it, and then you make the conscious decision to shift it to the next task. This is a critical practice that one should get mastery over. You will be good at whatever you practise.

Devote yourself to giving your undivided attention to each of your engagements, from the moment you rise to when you retire at night. Track your progress, you are doing this for you.

The better your ability to focus, the more meaningful interactions with the people you are with. You will be able to achieve a hundred percent because you can focus. You can listen better because you can focus better. When you focus better you can experience that moment better. The outcome is that you feel you are living a truly rewarding life. With concentration, your observation improves.

Willpower

Willpower channels all your energies towards one given point for a given length of time. Willpower helps to bring awareness back every time it drifts away. The more you use your willpower, the more you develop it. The willpower you develop will always remain with you and is always available for you to draw upon. Nothing in life happens without a will. A single point of focus to accomplish any goal is possible with willpower.

To develop willpower practise the following three methods.

1. Finish what you Start.
2. Finish it well, beyond your expectations, even though it takes more time.
3. Do slightly more than you think you can.

When each moment is used intentionally, life becomes fulfilling and rewarding. Willpower helps not only manifesting the life you want, but also in experiencing higher states of consciousness and ultimately self-realisation.

Conscious and Subconscious Minds

The mind has two levels: the conscious level and the subconscious level. You think with your conscious mind, and your subconscious mind records what you think with your conscious mind. Any continuous concept retained in the conscious mind must be brought into reality by the subconscious mind.

When the subconscious mind accepts a concept, it begins to carry it out. The subconscious mind is capable of processing both positive and negative ideas. Whatever you declare mentally and consciously as truth, your subconscious mind will accept and bring into your reality. What you thought in your conscious mind is replicated in your subconscious mind. You have the ability to choose.

Your conscious mind is the reasoning mind, it is that phase of the mind which chooses. You make all your decisions with your conscious mind. Your subconscious mind accepts what is impressed upon it or what you consciously believe. Your subconscious mind is like the soil which accepts any kind of seed, good or bad, it responds according to the nature of your thoughts or suggestions.

Your conscious mind is "the watchman at the gate." Its chief function is to protect your subconscious mind from false impressions. The subconscious mind simply reacts to the impressions given to it by your conscious mind. It cannot reason out like your conscious mind, it cannot argue logically. If you give wrong suggestions, it will accept them as true. All things that happened to you are based on thoughts that were impressed on your subconscious mind.

If you think favourably, positivity is stored in the subconscious mind; if you practise distraction, it is recorded in the conscious mind, and repetition records it in the subconscious mind. You should be extremely cautious about what you repeat, whether consciously or unintentionally.

What happens in the conscious mind is registered by the subconscious mind. The subconscious mind's concentration will regulate the awareness that is centred in the conscious mind. With increased attention, the conscious mind re-impresses the subconscious mind. A good attention cycle has begun.

Whenever you are not in charge of your awareness, then your subconscious governs where your awareness is going. Depending on the patterns you created, your subconscious will govern your awareness in a concentrated way or in a distracted way.

You see and feel what you expect to see and feel. The world you know is a picture of your expectations. If you want to enhance your performance or alter your behaviour in any area of your life, you must simultaneously embrace the mental picture of that accomplishment and hold onto it tightly as an imagined final result.

Whatever your conscious mind assumes and believes to be true, your subconscious mind will accept and bring it into your experiences. Your internal dialogue creates pictures and feelings that are stored in the subconscious mind and it starts influencing your future behaviour.

If you are unhappy with your experience, you must alter the nature of your conscious thought and expectations. You must change the signals you give to your subconscious mind by your thoughts and words to your acquaintances and contacts.

Your subconscious mind is a servant who is available to you 24 hours a day, seven days a week. It is objective; it does not tell you if you are making a good or terrible decision. It just executes the commands supplied to it by its superior, the conscious mind. So be aware of what ideas are going on in your conscious mind at all times, and if any negative thoughts arise, instantly convert them to good ones.

Your subconscious mind is the one with infinite intelligence and boundless wisdom. Whatever you impress upon your subconscious mind, the same will become real and practical. Therefore, you must impress the subconscious mind with the right ideas and constructive thoughts.

My Experiment

- I became very careful and started keeping an eye on my internal thoughts, because my thoughts are creating my life.

- By keeping my awareness 100% on whatever I am doing; I have improved my concentration.

- Wherever and whatever I am doing I am focused. I am living and experiencing my life without missing even a moment.

- Playing with children means playing with undivided attention.

- For the last 15 years I never carried my phone while I was walking or doing yoga. I keep my environment as less distractive as possible.

- I listen to others with 100% concentration.

Insights

- You can't see the mind with your eyes. The mind is a vast space.

- You are pure awareness moving in different areas of the mind.

- Everything is energy and vibrates at a certain frequency. Where awareness goes; energy flows.

- Awareness is nothing but concentrated energy.

- Concentration is the ability to keep awareness on one thing until you decide to move it onto something else.

- Will power is channelling all energies towards one given point for a given length of time.

- Will power can be developed by practice. Finish what you start, finish it well beyond your expectations and do a little more than you think you can.

- Your conscious mind is the reasoning mind and you take all your decisions with this.

- The subconscious mind simply reacts to the impressions given to it by your conscious mind.

- The subconscious mind registers what is going on in the conscious mind.

- Whatever you impress on your subconscious mind, it brings into your experience.

Action steps

(Read First and then Practise)

- Close your eyes
- Bring your first three fingers together (by doing this the brain slows down and shifts to the state before sleep) of both hands separately and keep on your thighs with your spine straight.
- Deeply inhale and slowly exhale for three times to bring balance to your breath.
- Now focus your awareness on your brain-stay for a few seconds.
- Shift awareness to your neck and shoulders-stay for a few seconds.
- Shift your awareness to your heart and chest-stay for a few seconds.
- Shift your awareness to your stomach-stay for a few seconds.
- Shift your awareness to your spine-stay for a few seconds.
- Shift your awareness to your thighs-stay for a few seconds.
- Shift your awareness to your knees-stay for a few seconds.
- Shift your awareness to your feet-stay for a few seconds.

- By keeping your awareness on a particular body part, you are energising that part. You can do this practise in as much detail as you wish.
- Where your awareness goes, energy flows there.
- You can also practise, by shifting your awareness from one place to the other and keep it as long as you wish for improving concentration.

Say to yourself –

- I am the awareness. I am feeling it.
- I am keeping my awareness with full concentration on any given work.
- I am developing my willpower by finishing what I started and finishing it well.
- I give thanks to the universe for providing me with the knowledge on awareness.
- Open your eyes, rub your palms, feel the heat and place your palms on your face and deeply inhale. Great.

To increase your will power:

I. Practise keeping your awareness on activities, which you are doing daily without missing, like –

    a. Make your bed-Fold your blanket and make your bed.

    b. Brushing your teeth-keep your awareness along the movement of the toothbrush.

- c. Bathing–Keep your awareness on your hands till you finish.
- d. Smiling–Watch yourself smiling in front of the mirror with awareness.
- e. Eating–Keep your awareness on the food you are eating and on chewing.
- f. Listening–Listen to others with 100% awareness.

II. Identify those activities which you have started but not finished. List out and focus on finishing them.

_____

_____

_____

_____

_____

_____

_____

_____

_____

_____

3
Self-Talk

What are you telling yourself ?

How you speak to yourself is one of the most important factors that have a profound impact on every element of your life. You listen to yourself more than anyone else during your life. The majority of your internal speech is unnoticed, what you tell yourself has the biggest impact on you. Your self-talk shapes your self-image, which influences your actions and accomplishments. So be aware of your self-talk. Your self-talk can determine your wealth, love, happiness, attractiveness, and strength or weakness.

Your current mental programming is created based on your past experiences, your acceptance of what you heard from others and your self-talk. What could you accomplish if you had the ability to completely remove the subconscious programmes that work against you and replace them with a fresh, empowered programme of unwavering belief and a new programme that will begin operating almost automatically in your favour ?

What exactly is Self-Talk ?

The script you employ to shape your life is the self-talk you have with yourself. If you send out negative messages all the time, your mind will eventually absorb them, which will cause you to think negatively and act negatively. Conversely, when you have constructive interactions, you start to view the world more favourably, which ultimately makes you feel better about yourself. You become the living result of your thoughts.

You cannot control the events in your life, but you can control how you react to them. Self-talk is essential for sustaining a really optimistic attitude on life.

When you engage in some positive self-talk, your confidence rises to new heights. Self-talk allows you to set your doubts aside so you can focus on attaining your goals. Positive self-talk can help you overcome shyness and a poor self-image. Negative thoughts frequently keep you from functioning to your best potential. Your degree of confidence is crucial to your success because it allows you to move forward boldly.

Check your programming

Since the day you were born, your indoctrination has been shaped, and the majority of your beliefs about who you are and the world around you got drilled into you. Whether the programming was accurate or wrong, true or false, your beliefs have been created as a result. Your programming sets the tone for everything. It is inevitable that the things you ingested or fed yourself with have resulted in a natural cause-and-effect chain reaction sequence that led to either successful self-management or an unsuccessful self-management.

Programming generates beliefs, which in turn generate attitudes and feelings, determine behaviours and repercussions. If you want to be more in charge of yourself, start by changing your programming. Without a doubt, if you allow other people to programme you in a way that matches their preferences, you are no longer in control.

Each day you may use different types of self-talk.

Level I-Negative talk

You are unknowingly accepting this negative self-talk. This self-talk is when you criticise or say anything unfavourable about yourself and then accept it.

Examples:

"I can't" or "I wish I could,"

"I could never accomplish that" "This just isn't my day."

These are common types of doubts, anxieties, misgivings, and hesitations you programme yourself with.

Level II-Although it acknowledges a problem, it offers no solution.

Examples:

I wish I could make more money, but I could not !

I wish I could, but I'm not able to.

I know I should take care of it, but I'm not taking care of it.

I wish things could turn out better, but they can't.

It is the instruction you are offering to yourself without being aware.

Level II self-talk always produces deep regret, disappointment, and acceptance of one's own imagined inadequacies.

Level III-In this, you acknowledge the need for change while also deciding to take action. Also, you express the choice in the "present tense" as though the change has already occurred.

Examples:

I no longer struggle to interact with co-workers. I never overindulge in food.

In traffic, I never get frustrated.

I don't put off anything that I want to get done.

When you advance to level III, you naturally start rephrasing previous negative "cannots" to communicate to your subconscious mind that it is time to get up, get going, and make the change. Regardless of what you tell the subconscious mind to do, it just follows your orders as it listens and waits for them.

If you tell something to the subconscious mind for a long enough period and with enough force, it will believe you. It will merely start working to implement its new instructions. You instruct the subconscious mind for it to function. It will comply if you learn how to communicate with it properly.

Level IV-At this level, you present the subconscious mind with a brand-new image of who you actually wanted to be, telling it to develop that version of you. You are saying to it "Forget about any bad programming I ever gave you. Your new programme is this."

Examples:

I have a well-organised, healthy, and energetic life and I make the right decisions.

I appreciate completing tasks. I have a great memory.

I am the winner.

Level IV self-talk instils you with confidence and firmly grounds you on the rock-solid foundation of achievement. That is the kind of self-talk that will motivate you, effect the changes you want to see, and set you on the path to realising your dream.

Positive Thinking:

Simply decide to think only positively from this point onwards throughout your life.

The ideas you live with longer are the ones you find more comfortable. Throwing out all bad thoughts is crucial, but it's equally important to replace the old with the new-word for word, thought for thought.

Positive thinking can only succeed with the proper kind of self-talk; otherwise, it only amounts to wishful thinking. Your awareness helps you in achieving your objectives.

You are consciously in charge of every change you make within yourself when you engage in active, daily self-talk. "You are your thoughts" . Think for yourself, talk for yourself, and programme your mind with your preferred options. Nobody should do that for you. Nobody else has the authority.

"Give me more," the human brain says. Please provide the wording. Give me the instructions, directives, picture, timetable, and desired outcomes, and I will carry them out for you. Please give me the words."

How does your brain function ?

Your brain will precisely execute your commands. If you tell negative things or positive things about yourself frequently and firmly the brain accepts it. It cannot distinguish between being wealthy or poor, good or bad. The brain accepts programming in the form that you provide. It has no choice. What you think is what you become.

One common example of this is your very own self-accepted idea about your financial capabilities or limitations. Unless you alter the programme, you gave yourself, the one that said you can't seem to generate enough money, your subconscious mind will be effective in carrying out its programmed purpose of preventing you from earning as much money as you desire. If correctly programmed, the subconscious mind would make you as rich as you desire.

Your subconscious mind keeps working nonstop to ensure that you perform exactly as you have consciously or unconsciously describe yourself. Only you have the power to control your unconscious ideas. Immediately begin employing your positive self-talk as part of your everyday practice.

Self-talk is a technique for erasing or replacing your old, harmful programming with deliberate, new programming. By talking to yourself differently and intentionally with more productive phrases and statements, you can send new instructions to your subconscious mind.

Techniques to improve Self-Talk:

The techniques that make self-talk work so well are easy and simple to use. There are five different methods for improving self-talk; you may use some or all of them.

1. Silent Self-Talk:

This is the self-talk that goes on all the time. You are typically unaware of it. Silent self-talk can be either a conscious or unconscious internal dialogue. This is the simplest and most natural technique to adopt when starting to replace negative self-talk with positive self-talk. When you talk to yourself out loud, use level III and level IV positive self-talk. It is a simple adjustment that requires more awareness than effort.

Silent self-talk includes anything and everything you think about yourself or the world around you. You should tell yourself that today is a great day to be alive and it is the time to start going with your new self-talk. Most of the things you consider problems are just perceptions; your perspective on each of them decides whether they really are a problem or not; All you need to do is tell yourself to see things in a better way.

Your old programming will try to argue with you when you start rephrasing your self-talk from the old to the new. As a result, when you begin, let's begin by deciding to ignore the earlier negative program that tries to convince you that it won't work. Keep in mind that this old self-talk is a habit because it feels comfortable and natural, even when it is negative. Knowing what to anticipate will enable you to confront negative self-talk head-on, overcome it, and start forming a new habit.

Listen to everything you say to yourself during the day. Any thoughts or statements you make to yourself that come off as negative self-talk should be noted in your mind, and they should be quickly reversed and replaced with positive ones.

Example:

"I just can't seem to get organised today". Immediately change it to –

"I am organised and in control".

"I really have got a problem with this". Turn around and say –

"I can handle this. I am a capable person".

"I just can't seem to lose weight". Change it to -

"Losing weight is never a problem for me. I eat exactly what I should and only the right and healthy amount. I am losing weight and looking good".

Although many of the messages you give yourself through silent self-talk may not be obvious, the brain still reacts right away and has an effect. By substituting fresh commands for your prior negative self-talk, you activate constructive, healthy electrical impulses in your brain that will naturally work for you rather than against you.

2. Self-Speak:

Your self-speak includes everything you say to yourself, to others about yourself, or about anything else.

Your spoken words play a very significant role. It directly impacts your subconscious mind. All of us will have some unpleasant situations in life where we feel obligated to put up with them. But it is entirely up to us whether we allow that circumstance to work against us or decide mentally to interpret it differently.

Every day, you make hundreds of statements. Each of these statements command your subconscious mind. When those statements are added up over the course of a week, month, or year, they amount to tens of thousands of minor but crucial subconscious self-directions that have a significant impact on your actions, emotions, and who you become.

Use self-talk to cultivate a mindset that yields winning outcomes. If 'positive self-talk' is practised regularly, it gets transformed into a regular ritual like eating and sleeping. When you speak, pay attention to everything you say. The best gift you can ever give to yourself is the positive self-talk. It is a treasure that you will never lose once you have mastered it. It enriches you day by day.

3. Self-Conversation:

Self-conversation is an art of speaking as if two people are speaking to each other.

Example:

Person 1-"You look amazing today ! You feel great, you're in great shape, and you're ready for anything !" and after that, respond by saying.

Person 2-"Yes, I feel good ! I feel great. I appreciate who I am, I'm happy to be alive, and today is a special day. It actually works.

You are playing the roles of both persons.

You can ask questions and receive straightforward answers when you talk to yourself aloud. You have a dear friend inside you who has been patiently waiting to hear from you.

4. Self-write :

Self-write is nothing but writing self-talk in verbatim.

Self-write is a powerful tool for reprogramming phrased on specific self-talk statements that deal with the most crucial new instructions you want to give your subconscious mind and the new programming you want to work on most, is known as self-write.

You start by scripting self-talk for each area of personal self-improvement. Create a daily ritual of reading the script to yourself. This is the practical approach in transforming self-talk to work effectively. It provokes thought, directs your attention, and engages you in the process of reprogramming your subconscious mind with new ideas very actively.

5. Record-the self-talk:

Recording self-talk is the most useful tool for every one of us.

Whether you are consciously listening to it or not, your subconscious mind will be busy in programming the positive new knowledge about you, as you listen to the recordings.

Start using just one of the techniques, which you feel most comfortable with. Go ahead and try something else if you want to. The other self-talk techniques just naturally fit into place once one of them starts to work for you.

Self-talk should be in the Present Tense.

All positive self-talk is always expressed in the present tense when it is written, read, recorded, listened to, or thought of. The desired modification is always presented as having already occurred. By doing this, you are presenting your subconscious mind with a finished image of the task completed. Your subconscious mind will follow your instructions more precisely and deliver whatever you instruct. Because it cannot distinguish between what is present and what is past.

Make a list of all the things you want to improve.

Examples:

I can accomplish whatever objective I set for myself.

I work out frequently.

I appreciate and have faith in myself.

I only consume what is appropriate.

I can listen well.

I enjoy my family time.

My Experiment

- I always keep an eye on what I am saying internally. If any negative talk surfaces immediately I replace it with a positive talk.

- Example: "I can't afford" immediately changing into "I can afford".

- You won't get-you will get.

- I am feeling uneasy-No, I am comfortable and feeling good.

- It doesn't happen-It will happen, I am experiencing a positive outcome.

- He is bad-No, He is good and he behaves well with me.

- In traffic feeling of delay-I will be on time for the scheduled meeting.

- Lack of money-I am receiving money and fulfilling my commitments.

Insights

- Your self-talk shapes your self-image.
- What you talk internally, is fed to your subconscious mind and is delivered.
- You have a choice to correct your self-talk by replacing it with new self-talk.
- What you think is what you become.
- Decide to think Positively throughout your life with the right self-talk.
- Self-talk can be corrected by 5 different methods:
    - Silent Self-Talk
    - Self-Speak
    - Self-Conversation
    - Self-Write
    - Record-Talk

Action steps

- First Assess your level of self-talk on different areas of your life.

Level	I.	II.	III.	IV.
On your appearance				
On your life partner				
On your work				
On your house				
On your vehicle				
On your finances				
On your children				
On your health				
On spirituality				
On the world around you				

- Now you have identified the level of yourself-talk in different areas of your life.

- Based on the level, identify the corrected self-talk against each area and write here.

- Note-Wording should be in the present tense, as if you have already received the desired outcome to impress upon your subconscious mind.

On your appearance–Example: I love my appearance

_____

_____

_____

_____

_____

On your life partner –

_____

_____

_____

_____

_____

On your work –

_____

_____

_____

_____

_____

On your house –

On your vehicle –

On your finances –

On your children –

On your health –

On spirituality –

On the world around you -

_____

_____

_____

_____

Now you have identified the right self-talk for you. Great. You are halfway through.

- Now Identify the method you would like to use for practice.

- **Silent self-talk**-silently use all new self-talk internally on each area of your life.

- **Self-speak**-say to yourself loudly all your new self-talk

- **Self-conversation**-converse with yourself with both ends aloud with new self-talk.

- **Self-write**-write new self-talk on each area to impress on your subconscious mind.

- **Record-talk**-Record with your voice all new self-talk on your phone and listen to it at least 2 to 3 times a day.

- You can choose all of the above; depending on your comfort and how fast you want to impress on your subconscious mind and have it start working for you.

WORKSHEET

4
Core Values

Core values are nothing but believing in some principles which enhance your quality of thinking and living. Core values guide and transform you into a powerful personality.

What values do you hold? Have you ever given it some thought as to which principles mean the most to you? Many of us are aware of the things that are important to us and the principles that influence our choices. We can have a better understanding of what our values actually are if we take some time to consider what is significant to us and why ?

Core values assist you in setting priorities, making choices and helping you to stay on a course, which will be in consistent with your needs and beliefs. Core values are nothing but a compass for your life.

Your core values make you invent and reinvent yourself.

They act as guides for your crucial decisions.

You will have a sense of equilibrium when your actions are consistent with your values. You will feel more at ease in the world by understanding what is important to you, and why it is essential. And how you incorporate them into your daily life is important. You don't need to worry about other people since you already know what's important to you.

Here is a list of core values. These can be applied to both your personal and professional life. This list might serve as an inspiration in deciding your own essential set of values. It is advisable to have three to five core values to focus on.

- Respecting everyone
- Being truthful to yourself
- Keeping your promises
- Relationships
- Creativity
- Growth
- Wisdom
- Optimism
- Joy
- Responsibility
- Respect
- Humility
- Acceptance
- Hard work
- Peace
- Success
- Trustworthy
- Serving others
- Respecting others
- Family oriented
- Focus
- Happiness
- Kindness
- Patience
- Freedom
- Spirituality
- Integrity
- Honesty
- Friendship
- Knowledge
- Power
- Wealth

My Experiment

- My core values have helped to guide me whatever the circumstances in my life. My core values are :

1. Respecting everyone.

2. Being trustworthy.

3. Delivering what I promise.

4. Being truthful to myself.

5. Serving others.

Insights

- Core values are some principles which enhance your quality of thinking and living.
- Core values assist you in setting priorities.
- Core values are like a compass for your life.

Action steps

- List out your core values. Write why those are important to you against each one. By writing this you are feeding information to your subconscious mind so that it reprograms and sees that you stick to your core values.

1.

_____

_____

_____

_____

2.

_____

_____

_____

_____

3.

_____

_____

_____

_____

4.

_____

_____

_____

_____

5.

_____

_____

_____

_____

6.

_____

_____

_____

_____

7.

_____

_____

_____

_____

5

Understanding Success

Success is not the same for any two people. It varies, and cannot be compared because everyone is created as a unique individual.

Success is identifying the life experiences you would like to have and working towards those with your maximum potential.

In the process, you and others will benefit. Enjoy the journey of success.

You will achieve your best by clearly understanding the meaning of success. Every one of us has a unique purpose, for which we are created by the universe. Your greatest joy lies in identifying... and working towards fulfilling it. No one else in the world has exactly the same gifts, talents, background or future. It is a serious mistake if you're trying to be someone other than yourself !

Think about your unique abilities and discover the desire of your heart. You will be successful, if you are willing to work towards reaching your potential. Your potential is the universe's gift to you and your return gift is what you do with the gifted potential. You have limitless potential. Very few try to reach it. You can do anything but you can't aspire to do everything. Don't allow people around you to decide the agenda for your life. It's your life, so find out exactly what is the deep desire of your heart is.

Only you can identify what it is that the universe wants to express through you. Once you've identified it, concentrate on that to reach your potential. You need to focus all your attention on it. There can be no success without sacrifice. If you desire to achieve only a little, sacrifice only a little. You will achieve more, if you are willing to sacrifice more.

With continuous improvement you can utilise your potential. Continuous improvement is the key to happiness. Happiness gives success. Reach a step closer to your potential each day. Today, you feel a little better than yesterday.

Forget the past ! The past is gone. You can't gain any momentum from it. Don't let your past prevent you from reaching your potential. Success can be measured by the obstacles which one has to overcome while trying to succeed. Focus on the future-your potential lies ahead of you. Whether you are 20, 35, 50 or 70, you still have room to improve yourself and become successful.

Success is different for every person, but the principles of the journey are the same.

My Experiment

- For me, success is living the life as on my own terms.
- Enjoying the journey of success by not being attached to the end results.
- Create balance in my life by enjoying all segments.
- Achieving my goals without compromising my Joy, peace and freedom.
- Success for me is how joyful I am and keeping the people around me joyful.

Insights

- Success is not the same for any two people.
- Your potential is the universe's gift to you and your return gift is what you do with the gifted potential.
- Enjoy the journey of success.
- It's your life. Find out what is the deep desire of your heart is.
- Continuous improvement is the key to happiness.

Action steps

- Deeply inhale and exhale. Relax.
- Bring balance to your breathing.
- Write here, what success means for you.

6
The Dream About Your Life

A dream provides you with a direction, acting as a compass for your journey. Moving in any direction other than towards your dream means missing out on the opportunities essential for success.

Every one of you, from the youngest to the oldest, has a dream placed in the depth of your heart. It's not just a fleeting wish or a passing fantasy but a profound vision that you are born to do.

This vision is often linked to your individual talents and unique gifts you possess. This leads you to your destiny. The journey to success starts with the power of your dream. A dream does many things for you. You all need something worthwhile to aim for.

A dream amplifies your potential. Without it, you may not look beyond your circumstances. However, with a dream, you enhance your capabilities, stretching every opportunity and resource. Your growth and development are channelled towards this dream. The dream creates a massive potential. A dream not only gives you hope for the future but also empowers you in the present. Dreams assist you in prioritising your actions.

There is a marked difference between those who dream and those who manifest their dreams. Everyone gets an idea, but only who acts upon it will be successful. Idea is nothing if you do not act upon it. A dream comes from a deep desire. Many discover their dream by an insight or motivated by their past.

If you're struggling to identify your dream, the following steps might guide you:

1. Believe in Your Ability to Succeed

You must believe that you have the potential to succeed. Realising your dreams is possible even if you're not a genius, blessed with luck, or affluent. The essential element is to believe that it can happen. The tools you are going to learn and practise from this book will help you in realising your dreams.

2. Overcome Pride and Self-Satisfaction

Self-Satisfaction can hinder progress and suffocate your dreams. Therefore, it's crucial to overcome your pride, which prevents you from trying new things out of fear.

Pride makes you stay in your comfort zone and discourage risk-taking. Yet, risk-taking is vital in the journey to realising your dream.

3. Break Free from Habitual Thinking

Habit is something you do without conscious thinking. This autopilot behaviour can sabotage dreams. And stop you from questioning and dreaming. It makes you accept the status quo without considering the realm of possibilities. Review all the things you're currently doing out of habit, shake things up, broaden your horizons, nurture your potential, initiate changes, and be creative. Begin an inward journey to discover your dream.

Realising a successful dream is a process that requires emotional investment. Your dream should grow beyond your thoughts and carry over into your feelings.

Committed action differentiates a successful dreamer from a mere daydreamer. Once you discover your dream, pursue it and commit to it until it materialises. The ability to achieve your dream may be closer and easier than you anticipate. It demands dedication and perseverance and necessitates weathering doubts and criticisms from those closest to you. However, you can achieve it.

A dream gives you a reason to venture forth, a path to follow, and a target to aim for. Without a clear destination, you might end up somewhere unintended. Once you identify your dream or purpose, it's crucial to constantly progress towards your dream. Setting specific goals is the best way to ensure that you stay on course.

My Experiment

- I dream about how I should appear, how to be spiritual, materialistic, how much to give back to society and this helps me how to run my day.

- I pursue my dreams and their practical aspects. I also analyse my core strengths in manifesting the dreams. Then start working on building a great team for attaining the desired outcome.

- I keep a clear vision on the end results of my goals to live my dream life.

- Once I get a positive feel that this is the right desire for me then I believe and expect the outcome. My expectancy transforms into reality.

Insights

- The journey of your success starts with the power of your dreams.
- Dreams assist you in prioritising your actions.
- Believe that it can happen.
- Your inward journey helps you to discover your dream.
- Constantly progress towards your dream with committed actions.

Action steps

To get started on the success journey the first step you need to take is to discover the dream of your life. Set aside several hours on weekends or maybe even a day off to work on the following material as honestly as you can.

1. My Past: Dreams comes out from life. Answer these questions.

    a) What are my greatest talents ?

    _____

    _____

    _____

    b) What is my greatest character ?

    _____

    _____

    _____

    c) What do others say that I am good at ?

    _____

    _____

    _____

d) What are my unique life experiences ?

_____

_____

_____

e) What is my greatest passion-which I am glad to do for free ?

_____

_____

_____

f) What is so important to me, even willing to die for it ?

_____

_____

_____

2. **My Present:** looking at present circumstances don't be discouraged, it is part of the process of discovering your dream. Answer these questions to see the potential of the present:

   a) What are all my current resources? (time, money, people, opportunities, etc.)

   _____

   _____

   _____

b) To free up more resources or to create more opportunities; what should I positively change in current circumstances ?

_____

_____

_____

c) What is the uniqueness of the current circumstances–the place where I live, where I work, the people I know or what is that ?

_____

_____

_____

3. **My Future:** You are beginning to see patterns created by your past and present circumstances. Now you decide how you want to create your dream life. Write that here.

_____

_____

_____

With what you will learn from later chapters you will start moving closer to achieving your dream life.

WORKSHEET

7

Setting Your Goals

Setting goals is a fundamental aspect of human nature. This propels you forward, drives your ambitions, and gives meaning to your life. Whether in personal, academic, or professional spheres, goals act as guiding beacons, directing your efforts towards a desired destination. Understanding the power of setting goals can lead to increased productivity, enhanced motivation, and ultimately, a more fulfilling life.

The Significance of Goal Setting

By defining what you want to achieve, you create a clear vision of your future. This vision acts as a powerful motivator, encouraging you to push beyond your comfort zones and strive for growth.

Moreover, goals provide structure and direction to your achievements. Without specific goals, you wander aimlessly, not sure of where you are headed. Goals act as compass points, guiding you on your journey, and helping you make decisions aligned with your long-term aspirations.

Goal setting also enhances your sense of purpose and self-esteem. When you achieve your goals, no matter how big or small, you experience a sense of accomplishment and fulfilment. This positivity reinforces further your determination and encourages you to set even higher goals.

What is the definition of a goal ?

"A goal is the ongoing pursuit of a worthy objective, until accomplished."

'Ongoing' denotes a process since goals take time to achieve. Pursuit suggests that there might be a chase involved; 'worthy' suggests that the chase will be valuable. And that the reward will be sizable enough. It implies that you will do whatever it takes to complete the task till it is done. Set your goals through your soul-searching process. You will understand your inner energy better and what it truly wants to experience through you. Reaching the goals helps you in identifying your life's purpose.

Checklist for setting goals effectively:

1. Your most important goals must be yours:

You should ask yourself. "What do I really want to experience ?".

Only you can understand, no one else. This is because your mind, which is the storage of your previous actions, will help you in identifying your future actions based on your previous actions.

You are sabotaging your future, when you let other people or society determine your definition of success without having an awareness of your conscious desire. Please put a stop to that right away.

One of the biggest forces that affects you is the media. The way you dress, the vehicles you drive, the places you live, and the vacations you take; are all used by the media to define success. Your reputation is either successful or unsuccessful based on how you perform in these categories.

Decide right now to define success according to your standards and stop caring what other people think. Set personal goals based on your inner voice and pay no attention to what society says about you.

If you really want to drive a luxury car or live in a beautiful home or create an exciting lifestyle; just go for it ! Just make sure that's what you really want, and that you are doing it for the right reasons.

2. Your Goals must be Meaningful:

Ask yourself the following questions as you get ready to write down your future goals:

"What is essential to me ?"

"What is the purpose of achieving this ?"

"What am I prepared to give up making this happen ?"

Clarity will improve through this method of thinking.

What are the perks and advantages of this new discipline, you could ask yourself? Concentrate on the brand-new, thrilling lifestyle that you can experience by taking persistent action. If this does not excite or give you an adrenaline rush, it is not the right goal, and you should search for the right goal.

The goal is your choice, and you are accountable for each decision you make, therefore choose wisely. Set goals now that will lead you to future success, joy, independence, and peace of mind.

3. Your Goals must be Specific and Measurable:

Define your goals clearly. Weak generalisations and casual statements are not good. As an illustration, consider the statement,

"My goal is to be financially independent."

What exactly does that mean? Being financially independent for some people means having $100 million in safe investments.

Or it may be earning $50,000 annually. Or being debt-free.

What exactly is it for you? What is the exact number you are looking for? Take the time to determine right away if this is a goal that is significant to you.

"My goal is to spend more time with my family."

This is another illustration. This lacks clarity. (How much time, when, how often, what you will do with it, and with whom? To be more specific, you need to have more clarity.)

The formulation of a goal like "Start exercising," which is too general. It cannot be measured in any manner.

Change the phrase to

"I want to exercise 30 minutes a day, five times a week."

Repeat this question numerous times to be more specific. The health goal should be like :

"Workout from Monday to Friday, from 6.00am to 6.30am for 30 minutes a day, five times a week". Stretching for 10 minutes and cycling for 20 minutes makes the workout regime. You can now monitor the development. You are now responsible for the outcome.

Set a challenge for yourself when you make a goal. "Be more specific."

Repeat this until the objective is clear and measurable. By doing this, you'll improve your odds of getting the outcome you want. A non-measurable goal is nothing more than wishful thinking !

4. Your Goals must be Flexible:

You don't want to create a system that is overly tight and constrictive.

Example:

To prevent boredom when engaging in an exercise programme for better health, you may wish to change the timings during the week and the type of exercise.

A flexible strategy gives you the flexibility to alter your direction.

You would be crazy not to take advantage of a genuine opportunity when it comes across.

Remember that you don't have to get involved with every new concept; concentrating on one or two makes you content and successful.

5. Your Goals must be Challenging and Exciting:

When you establish interesting and challenging goals, you gain the advantage of not settling into a life of boredom. You must push yourself to leave your comfort zones to do this.

When you are uncomfortable, you always learn more about yourself and your ability to achieve. Aim high. Set objectives that make you so excited and sleepless. Life offers a lot, so why shouldn't you take advantage of it to the fullest ?

6. Your Goals must be in Alignment with Your Values:

The foundation for harmony is set in motion when your goals are consistent with your core values. What are your guiding principles? Anything that resonates with you deeply and about which you have strong feelings. These are solid, foundation ideas that have shaped your character for many years. For instance, honesty, integrity, and trustworthiness. Your gut instinct or intuition will remind you when your actions are inconsistent with your principles.

Making decisions is simple when you apply your basic principles to achieve positive, interesting, and worthwhile goals, if you are not hampered by internal disagreement. This sparks a wave of success that elevates you to much higher levels.

7. Your Goals must be Well-balanced and Integrated:

What would you do differently if you had to live your life over again? When people in their eighties are asked this question, they unmistakably respond that they would travel more, see their family more often, and have a lot more fun. Therefore, while you are making goals, be sure to include areas that allow for more downtime and enjoyment of life's finer things. Life is too short to miss the good stuff.

8. Your Goals must be Realistic:

Being realistic will help you achieve the best results. Most people are unrealistic in determining the timelines to accomplish their goals. Keep in mind that there are only unrealistic time frames; there are no unrealistic goals.

Example:

The likelihood that someone under four feet tall will never play professional basketball.

It is unrealistic to become a millionaire in three months if your annual income is $50,000.

So, think big and imagine at bright future with excitement. Just make sure you give yourself reasonable amount of time to get there.

9. Goals must include Contribution:

The underlying fact is that What a man sows, he will eventually reap. Giving forth excellent things ensures rewards in return.

There are different ways you can contribute. You may provide your time, your knowledge, and money. Include contribution to the society as part of your goals. Do it without hesitation. Don't expect immediate payback. It will eventually appear, in the most unexpected ways.

10. Your Goals need to be Supported:

There are three viewpoints.

First: Some people will announce their plans to the entire world in advance. They say that it increases their accountability. When you opt for this course of action, there is a lot of pressure. The benefit of having large aspirations is that they attract other big dreamers.

Second: Set your own goals. Keep them to yourself and focus on your work. Action speaks louder than words.

Third: This is possibly the best. Tell a few individuals you trust. These are proactive people that you have been carefully selected to help and inspire you when needed.

Your Master Plan

Designing the life of your dreams deserves a little bit of attention and planning. This is the big picture. For creating a better future with clarity here are seven major steps:

1. **Review your Goals:**

When you get down to designing your actual goals, refer to the checklist for setting goals as a guide. It will assist in creating an image that is quite clear.

2. **Decide what You want to Accomplish and Why:**

Make a list of everything you want to do over the next five years and be as open-minded as possible. Do not limit your ideas in any way. By beginning each statement with "I am" or "I will," you may be particular and make your list unique. As an example, I am taking a six-weeks' vacation every year or saving or investing 10% of my net monthly income.

For a healthy integrated lifestyle choose some goals in each of the following categories:

- Business / Profession.
- Financial.
- Enjoyment.
- Health and fitness.
- Relationships.
- Personal.
- Contribution.

Choose any others as well that are particularly important to you, to guarantee that you have a healthy and integrated lifestyle.

Write against each category what you want. Once you identify, the "what" ask yourself "why" you want it. If you are not able to convince your mind why you want that, then change the goal and keep asking the question until your mind accepts it. Because your mind is associated with your consciousness and knows your previous actions, it will guide you properly. Once you have a convincing answer for "why" you want it? then work on timelines-on "when" you want it.

3. **Prioritising Your List:**

Look at each of your goals and their realistic completion dates. You are now aware of which goals are one-, three-, and five-year goals. Setting priorities is the next stage. Put a number next to each goal. Your goals can be prioritised and that will make you aware of where to keep your attention.

Before you assign priorities write down the most significant motivation for each goal. Also write the reward for successful completion. The significant motivation against each goal keeps you going even during difficult times.

4. **Create Inspiring Pictures:**

Create motivating images of your most significant goals to improve your concentration on the new lifestyle you want. Finding images on the internet is very easy.

Example:

One of your priorities is to visit London and Paris. Find amazing photos of the places you want to visit and the things you want to do. Make a PowerPoint presentation. Also include encouraging phrases like, "I am enjoying a two-week trip to London and Paris." Include the date you intend to travel.

For your subconscious mind to actively participate, look at these images frequently. Goals can be accomplished by adding feelings or emotions with a strong belief.

5. Capture Your best Ideas:

Make a dedicated file on your laptop, iPad, or smartphone where you may keep all your brilliant ideas. Or simply jot down your thoughts in a small notebook. It helps you in increasing your awareness. Write down important ideas you have, even if you have them in the middle of the night. Otherwise, you might forget them.

Idea capturing is so valuable. By noting down your great ideas, you can avoid having to rely on your memory which also avoids strain on the brain. You are always free to revisit your ideas. Simply keep your eyes and ears alert every day and listen to your intuition. When you regularly connect with your emotions, you are aware of what is going on in your life.

6. Visualise:

By mastering the visualisation techniques, you can become a champion in your chosen area. Use your positive imagination to create desired outcomes of your goals. The sharper those images are and, the more intensely you feel them, the more likely you create the desired results.

7. Develop Mentors:

Take the help of people who have vast experience in the areas you need the most help. When you surround yourself with a carefully chosen team of experts, your progress in learning increases rapidly and the wisdom received from them propels you towards faster results.

My Experiment

- I have clear short term and long-term goals in each segment of my life and also for the projects I am working on.

- I review and revise my goals as and when I feel like it. I am not really bothered on exact timelines but I enjoy the journey and I stay focused on the end results.

- I always set end goals not on the means to end goals. When I start focusing, the people and, the situations show up in my life and help me towards attainment of my end goals. Timelines may vary, but success happens at the appropriate time.

- Whenever I set my goals as per my deep desire they get manifested.

- The size of the goal does not matter, because in the eyes of the universe everything is small. What matters was my own gut feeling and staying focused on end results.

Insights

- Goals propel you forward and drive your ambitions.
- Goals provide a clear vision for your future.
- Define your goals clearly.
- Your goals must be measurable.
- Create goals for the short-term and long-term. Set your goals based on your inner voice.
- Be flexible and not attached to the end results.
- Enjoy the journey of achieving the goals.

Action steps

- To enjoy a healthy integrated lifestyle, choose goals in each of the following areas.
    - Health and fitness, Career / Business, Finance, Family, Personal, Entertainment and contribution.
- The following questions will help you in getting clarity on setting your goals.
    - What do I want to do ?
    - What do I want to have ?
    - What do I want to learn ?
    - What do I want to become ?
    - Where do I want to go for entertainment ?
    - What to do, to have optimum health ?
    - What contribution do I want to make ?
    - How much do I have to earn and save ?
    - What are my family requirements ?
    - Where do I want to live ?
    - What vehicles do I want to use ?
    - Take a break from routine and work on your goals quietly.
    - Once you identify your goals in each segment check with the following approach whether

they are your ideal goals or need to work further.

What do you want–write your goal ?

_____

_____

_____

Why do you want this? Answer

_____

_____

_____

Why do you want this? Answer

_____

_____

_____

Why do you want this? Answer

_____

_____

_____

- If you can convince your mind that this is the goal, you want to achieve; finalise your goal.
- If not, modify the goal and repeat the process.
- Once you finalise your goal, work on achieving the goal.
- Prepare action steps and timelines against each of them and finally arrive at target date for achieving your goal.
- For each goal same process-What do you want ?

Why do you want it? How will you get there? When will you get there ?

After a detailed assessment write all your goals here–

_____

_____

_____

_____

_____

_____

_____

_____

_____

_____

U R A Creator

- You can have short-term (3 months to one year) and long-term goals (3, 5 & 10 years)

Goals	Time						
	Jan–Mar 20_ _	Apr–Jun 20_ _	Jul–Aug 20_ _	Sept–Dec 20_ _	20_ _	20_ _	20_ _
Family							
Health							
Career/Business							
Personal							
Financial							
Entertainment							

- I strongly recommend that you spend at least one day to complete the above critical action plan.

WORKSHEET

WORKSHEET

8

Your Commitment

You arrived on earth to perform your own deeds. You should start doing that right away. "Commitment" is crucial for this.

When you commit to anything, it automatically gets done. If for any reason you are unable to keep your commitment, then what you initially believed to be a commitment was just a promise or a plan that you were ultimately unable to carry out.

You must understand the distinction between a commitment and a promise or a plan. If you make a commitment, you should fulfil it.

If you tell yourself-I am committed to delivering this, then you will see the success of every project you work on. To reach a successful ending, you must rely on yourself. Offer no excuses or justifications. There are numerous justifications for not keeping your commitments, which ultimately lead to failure.

When you commit firmly entire nature starts supporting you. From the moment of commitment you will receive continuous stream of supporting events, incidents, individuals, and all valuable resources coming to your aid.

Once you decide and commit, others will respect you and view you as a powerful individual. By committing yourself, you have already been successful. You will get enormous power. How much..? As much as you need to keep your commitment.

Almost everyone faces hesitation, justifications, weaknesses, and failures. Most people fail in life because of the difficulty in judging what is right and what is wrong. This keeps you away from living in your true potential. Additionally, it traps you in a realm of "nearly" and "could have been."

Failure does not exist in the world of dedication. People misunderstand the experience of challenge as failure. You must be able to completely rely on yourself. You must resolve to overcome all challenges if you want to accomplish your goals. You will succeed when you are fully committed and have the right attitude.

When you are completely confident in yourself, you will display such strength and strong self-confidence that other people will trust and invite you to participate in their plans. You will be in high demand. People will be aware that they can rely on you. They'll naturally have faith in your judgement and skills.

Failure only happens when you give up. You are always working to fulfil your commitment up until that time.

The universe simply uses apparent setbacks and failures to strengthen your courage, tenacity, and desire to win. Just move forward.

My Experiment

- I committed to my core values. Because of commitment I always followed my value system.

- I committed to always think positively. If any negative thought comes, automatically it will be replaced with positive thought.

- I committed to take care of my physical body, which helped me in taking the right kind of food, in the right quantities and at the right intervals. I have been a vegetarian for the last 20 years.

- I am committed-that-means it is done.

- Once I am committed the universe starts helping me through in all means for manifestation.

Insights

- When you commit to anything, it automatically gets done.

- To reach a successful ending, you must rely on yourself.

- When you commit firmly entire nature starts supporting you.

- People misunderstand the experience of challenge as failure.

Action Steps

- List out the improvements that you are committed to, in a day-to-day life.

_____

_____

_____

_____

_____

- Write the list of goals you are committed to.

_____

_____

_____

_____

_____

- Write the action steps you are going to take against each goal you are committed to.

Example: Build 50 units of an apartment complex

Action Steps:

1. Finalise the location
2. Prepare the budget
3. Mobilise the working capital

4. Get drawings from the architect
5. Get approvals from govt. authorities
6. Get a bank loan sanctioned
7. Deploy the contractors
8. Create the sales plan
9. The work quality check
10. Handover the complex to the association of purchasers etc.

- Now write down your action steps against each goal you committed to.

_____

_____

_____

_____

_____

_____

_____

_____

_____

_____

_____

_____

Your Commitment

WORKSHEET

WORKSHEET

9

Developing Habits

Habit means-something that you do often and regularly, something that you are doing it without knowing. According to a study, habits are responsible for around 40% of our daily behaviour. Your present habits essentially make you who you are today. How physically fit or unfit are you? How contented or discontented you are; how successful or unsuccessful you are. Everything is a result of your habits.

When you learn to change your habits, you can change your life because what you repeatedly do (i.e., what you spend time thinking about and doing each day), eventually shapes who you are, what you believe, and how you present yourself.

Let's say maintaining excellent health is a high priority on your list of habits. Then setting a minimal standard of exercise and frequency each week will help keep you in shape. A "no exceptions policy" is the solution, which indicates that you will continue your workout routine regardless of what happens, since you value the long-term benefits.

Let's examine a different circumstance. Always set aside and invest at least 10% of your income. Consistently implementing this each month is an excellent habit. This

Developing Habits

is something you should tell yourself since it will improve your long-term financial independence program.

Your habits influence your destiny. People who are casual about change will give up after a few weeks or months. They typically have a long list of justifications for why it didn't work out for them as well. If you want to stand out from the crowd and lead a unique existence, understand this: your habits influence your destiny.

Successful individuals do not simply rise to the top. Making things happen requires daily effort, self-discipline, and focus. All that depends on your habits.

Your habits affect your quality of life, which include things like financial security, fulfilling relationships, maintaining good health, and finding a harmonious balance between work and personal life. Another key prerequisite is that you must know who you are.

Your life will flow more freely the more you understand that you are unlimited energy, that your thoughts determine how you feel and act, and that you are the universe's expression.

You start to make better decisions based on intuition and instinctively knowing what is the right thing to do rather than just working hard. Your daily quality of life is determined by this increased level of awareness. Regularly re-evaluating your options is a very healthy habit to acquire.

When a new habit takes root and matures, it eventually replaces your previous habits. You can develop a completely new method of doing things by layering a new habit on top of your current habit. Simply substituting your old habits with new successful habits, will suffice. For instance, if you always arrive late to meetings, resolve to arrive ten minutes early for all appointments over the following several weeks to address this. To keep yourself on track, you need to have a few internal conversations. Being on time gets simpler the more often you do it, almost like being reprogrammed.

You can significantly improve your way of life by methodically getting better at each activity one at a time. Your relationships, finances, health and fun are all included in this. Until you take action, nothing much will change in your life.

How to Identify Bad Habits:

Your routines, patterns and behaviours often go unnoticed. Here are a few common bad habits that are holding you back.

- Eating fast food regularly.
- Not attending to paperwork effectively and quickly.
- Not returning phone calls on time.
- Poor communication between colleagues and staff.
- Not exercising to stay fit and healthy.
- Hitting the snooze alarm in the morning before getting out of bed.
- Wasting time on the internet.

- Not spending enough time with children.
- Being glued to the phone while eating with life partner/family.
- Being late for meetings and appointments.
- Not taking enough time off for fun and family.
- Forgetting someone's name after being introduced.

Now review and compile a list of all the habits that hinder your productivity. It's challenging to develop more productive habits unless you have a clear understanding of what is holding you back.

To identify your habits, you can also ask for feedback. Speak with people you respect and appreciate who are familiar with you. When you engage in harmful habits, your outer behaviour is what they see, not what you think you are doing, which is frequently an illusion. If you are receptive to constructive criticism, you can quickly make changes and permanently get rid of undesirable habits.

Your behaviour is greatly influenced by your habits, which are the by-products of the environment you are exposed to.

You can begin to believe what other people say if you spend time with those who are constantly complaining about the state of things.

However, if you surround yourself with strong, upbeat individuals, you are more likely to view a world brimming with opportunities and adventure.

Your transformation can be aided by a great coach, teacher, mentor or a good role model; "you must commit to change", is the only pre-requisite.

How To Change Bad Habits?

Successful people have formed successful habits. Recognise these habits by observation. Study those who are successful. Take them out for breakfast or lunch and probe them about their routines, habits, and disciplines. What are they reading? How do they set up their schedule? Genuinely motivated individuals who are truly successful are happy to offer their insights.

Reading successful people's autobiographies and biographies is another way to learn about them. Another method is to listen to audio programmes that are instructive and inspirational as you exercise or walk. Videos, apps, and training materials for inspiration can be found online.

Living is a learning process. It doesn't stop. Learn to improve your habits all the time. You develop character when you continuously work to get better. You will constantly experience consequences for your choices in life. Until you change your habits, nothing will change.

There are 3 simple ways:

a) **Clearly Identify Bad or Unproductive Habits:**

It's crucial that you consider how your bad habits will affect you down the road. When you examine your ineffective behaviour on a given day, it might not seem so bad. But it all adds up. If you smoke ten cigarettes a day for twenty years, that's 73,000 cigarettes in total. The results could be fatal. Because of this, you should always consider the long-term effects when examining your own harmful habits. Be really honest; otherwise your life could be at stake.

b) **Define Your New Successful Habit:**

This is just the opposite of your bad habit. In a smoker's example, it would be 'not smoking'. The more you are understanding the advantages and rewards of your new successful habit, the more likely you will adopt it.

c) **Create An Action Plan:**

When the urge for a cigarette strikes in the smoking example, replace it with something else.

Read books on quitting smoking. Stay away from other smokers.

You must take action and start by changing just one habit at a time.

The following habits have helped me a lot:

- Constantly monitoring my self-talk.
- Waking up early.
- Setting clear goals and consistently working on them.
- Practising time management.
- Staying focused with clarity.
- Being a Self-Motivator.
- Setting short-term and long-term goals.
- Being a lifelong learner.
- Upgrading my existing skills.
- Learning from my mistakes.

My Experiment

- Waking up daily by 5 am, which helps me in taking care of my morning rituals like meditation, walking and doing yoga.
- I modified my eating habits which helped me in reducing medication up to 70% less.
- By practice I have habit of only positive thoughts even in adverse situations.
- I developed a habit of being on time for all my appointments.
- I cultivated a habit of reading for at least 30 minutes every day.

Insights

- Your habits make your life.
- Old habits can be replaced with new habits.
- Your behaviour is influenced by your habits.
- You must commit to change for developing new habits.
- Observe successful people's habits and take their insights.
- By changing your habits, you change your life.
- By understanding the advantages of a new habit, you are more likely to adopt it.
- Create an action plan for changing un-productive habits.

Action Steps

- List out your unproductive habits here

- List out your new successful habits here

- Write the advantages of every new habit

- Create an action plan for each new habit to convert it into a successful habit

WORKSHEET

10
The Power of Affirmations

Affirmations are positive statements that you consciously repeat to yourself to reinforce beliefs. By saying affirmations, you can purify your mind.

Affirmations help you in achieving the outcome you want. Your thoughts cannot be stopped but can be controlled. An affirmation is a tool to replace negative thoughts with positive ones. By saying affirmations, you can purify your mind.

In the journey of life, you often face challenges and uncertainties that can shake your confidence and test your resilience. Amidst the highs and lows, you may find yourself seeking a way to stay positive and focused on your goals. That's where the incredible power of affirmations comes into play.

Affirmations act as a beacon of light, guiding you through the darkest moments and reminding you of your inherent potential. Affirmations have the remarkable ability to transform your thoughts, emotions, and actions, making them invaluable tools for personal growth and self-improvement.

By incorporating affirmations into your daily routines, you can begin to rewire your subconscious mind, replacing self-doubt with self-assurance and negativity with positivity. When you declare "I am capable," "I am worthy," or "I am deserving," you cultivate a sense of self-belief that empowers you to embrace challenges as opportunities for growth rather than obstacles to your success. By focusing on the positive aspects of life, you attract abundance and opportunity, which further reinforces your belief in the power of affirmations.

It is crucial to remember that affirmations are not merely wishful thinking; they require a genuine belief in their truth. When you couple your affirmations with a strong faith in yourself and your abilities, you unlock a powerful force that propels you towards your goals. By internalising these positive messages, you create a harmonious alignment between your thoughts, feelings, and actions.

Consistency and repetition are keys for harnessing the full potential of affirmations. Like watering a plant daily, the regular practice of affirmations nurtures your confidence, courage, and resilience. The more you repeat these positive declarations, the deeper they sink into your subconscious, guiding you towards actions that support your aspirations.

Utilising affirmations simply entails expressing yourself in ways that clearly imply positive things about yourself. They reinforce in your mind that the claim you are making is already true. These affirmations penetrate the inner mind's belief systems through regular repetition and reminders, acting as personal mantras.

The manifestation of your goals is brought about by affirmations and visualisation with a powerful feeling of accomplishment.

The repetition of affirmations is a deliberate effort to switch out negative thoughts with positive ones. It can change how you see yourself and the world.

When writing the affirmation, use the first person present continuous tense. Describe the outcome you want as if it is already true. It's better not to use more than 15 affirmations at once, with each repetition occurring 3 to 5 times. The best times are right after you wake up in the morning and right before you go to bed at night.

Affirmations can be recited silently, aloud, in writing, or through song or chant. Positive affirmations may turn a bad-tempered person into a happy person, by just spending a few minutes each morning. Any uplifting comment can be an affirmation.

Examples of Self-Motivating Affirmations:

I feel good about myself: Accept everything about you and your situation that you cannot change easily or right away.

I believe in myself: Believing yourself is one of the best ways to inspire yourself.

I choose to be free: Let your sense of self-worth be the only factor influencing your personal happiness. Choose freedom.

I can: The best phrase for boosting self-confidence is, "I can achieve anything". Your energy level also rises when you say 'I can'.

I'm capable of anything: This affirmation is designed to boost your determination and self-assurance.

I enjoy who I am: Loving yourself is embracing who you are. Put to like yourself.

I have a strong sense of self-confidence: Self-confidence is one of the most significant qualities of your personality. It raises your self-confidence.

I am strong and healthy: This will encourage you to take care of your body by giving it the exercise, nutrition, and relaxation it needs.

Every day I am getting better and better: All of your secret hopes and desires are already stored in your brain. This statement will inspire you to do every activity that is required.

Everything is coming easily and effortlessly to me: This will help you live a life that is free from stress and worry.

Everything is working out well for me: You create the conditions for beautiful and happy outcomes by repeating this affirmation.

I am a radiant being full of love and laughter: A self-inspiring statement draws new individuals into your life.

I'm attracting prosperity, good fortune, and love into my life: You create the foundation for a glorious future filled with promise by repeating this statement.

Here are a few helpful points for writing affirmations :

When writing your affirmations, be quite, precise and meditative.

Keep your affirmations as clear, concise and targeted as you can.

Let only uplifting messages be conveyed in your statements. Pick adjectives and thoughts you genuinely believe in.

Include a genuine desire for something in your affirmation. Make sure you completely believe in what you are saying.

Acquire an understanding of the significance of consistent repetition.

Examples of day-to-day Affirmations:

- Now I am weighing 70 kgs. I am looking good and feeling good.
- I am enjoying perfect health and physical fitness.
- My blood pressure, blood sugar and eyesight are normal all the time.
- I am enjoying my time with my family and children.
- I am enjoying every moment of my life with joy, peace and freedom.

- I always have enough resources to deliver all my goals.
- I am a successful business man and my business is growing every day.
- My imaginative capacity is very powerful. Whatever positive aspect I am visualising,... I am receiving it.
- I am walking for 45 minutes, doing 45 minutes of physical activity and 20 minutes meditation 5 times a week. I am enjoying this.
- I am delivering my job responsibilities comfortably and with more ease.
- I am focused and spending time on achieving my goals
- I am thankful to the universe for whatever I already have and for giving me whatever positive things I am asking for.
- All my decisions are guided by the universe.

Depending on your goals, write your affirmations in the simple, present tense and repeat them aloud for the brain to register. Then the brain takes the responsibility to deliver.

My Experiment

- I have affirmations for my physical health, my spiritual practices, my business goals and my family goals.

- Every morning, I say my affirmations during walk. I repeat each affirmation 3 times, adding a beautiful feeling to the words.

- The day-to-day affirmations I listed as examples above, are same of the ones I actually use every day.

Insights

- Affirmations help you in achieving the outcome you want.
- Affirmations can purify your mind.
- Affirmations rewire your brain.
- Affirmations with visualisation and a feeling of accomplishment helps in manifesting your goals.
- Write your affirmations in the present continuous tense.

Action Steps

Example 1: Buying a car

- Now I am driving my new blue-coloured BMW 5 series car.

Example 2: Buying a house

- Now I am celebrating the house-warming ceremony for my 5-bedroom villa with my family and friends.

- Write Affirmations for each of your goals.

- Write Affirmations for each of your new successful habits.

11
The Power of Visualisation

Visualisation is the practice of imagining what you want to achieve in the future as if it is true today.

Visualisation is the process of using your mind and your imagination to create pictures, and ideas of any desired goal, outcome, or scenario that you want. The process of visualisation directs your subconscious mind to be aware of the end goal you have in the mind. The secret of successful visualisation lies in how intensely you believe in them.

Visualisation serves as a powerful tool for programming the subconscious mind, and increase as the likelihood of achieving the desired outcomes.

By defining specific, measurable, achievable, relevant, and time-bound goals, you will gain clarity about your aspirations and create a roadmap for success. Goal setting along with visualisation enhances motivation, focus, and belief in the attainment of the goals. It bridges the gap between the current reality and the desired future, allowing you to align your thoughts, emotions, and actions with your goals.

The Role of Your Subconscious Mind:

The subconscious mind plays a vital role in attaining your goals. It acts as a storehouse of beliefs, memories, and emotions that shape your thoughts and actions. When you visualise your goals, you tap into the power of the subconscious mind, which does not differentiate between imagined and real experiences. By repeatedly visualising the desired outcome, you can program the subconscious mind to align your thoughts, emotions, and behaviours with the goal, making it more likely to manifest in reality.

The Power of Mental Imagery and the Brain's Response:

Neuroscience research has shown that the brain responds to mental imagery like real experiences. When you vividly imagine a specific goal, the brain's neural networks associated with that experience are activated. This activation stimulates the release of neurotransmitters and hormones related to motivation, focus, and positive emotions, creating a neural blueprint that strengthens the neural pathways associated with the desired outcome.

Neuroplasticity and Rewiring the Brain through Visualisation:

Neuroplasticity refers to the brain's ability to reorganize and form new neural connections throughout our life time. Visualisation can leverage neuroplasticity to rewire the brain by reinforcing positive thoughts, beliefs, and behaviours associated with the desired goal. Regular and focused visualisation practices can strengthen the neural pathways related to the goal, making them more resilient and facilitating the achievement of the goal.

Principles of Effective Visualisation for Manifesting Goals

a) Be clear and be specific in Formulating your Goal:

When using visualisation to manifest goals, it is crucial to have a clear and specific understanding of what you want to achieve. Vague or general goals may result in scattered and unfocused visualisation. By clearly defining the desired outcome, including specific details, measurable milestones, and a timeline, you provide a framework for effective visualisation.

b) Clarity and Sensory Engagement in Visualisation:

To maximise the effectiveness of visualisation, it is essential to make the mental images as clear and detailed as possible. Engage all your senses to create a multisensory experience within your imagination. Visualise the sights, sounds, smells, tastes, and even the physical sensations associated with achieving your goal. The clearer and more immersive your visualisation, the more impactful it can be in programming your subconscious mind for success.

c) Emotional Resonance and Harnessing Positive Feelings:

Emotions play a significant role in visualisation and manifesting goals. When visualising your goal, tap into the positive emotions associated with its achievement. Feel the joy, excitement, and fulfilment that you would experience upon reaching your desired outcome. Emotions increase the likelihood of attaining your goal.

d) Consistency and Regular Practice:

Consistency and regularity are key to making visualisation an effective habit. Incorporate visualisation into your daily routine, ideally at a dedicated time and place. Consistent practice reinforces the neural pathways associated with your goal, deepening the connection between your visualisation and your desired outcome. Treat visualisation as an ongoing practice rather than a one-time exercise, and commit to regularly spending time on it.

e) Alignment of Beliefs and Self-Identity with the Desired Outcome:

Visualisation is not only about creating mental images but also about aligning your beliefs and self-identity with your desired outcome. Examine any limiting beliefs or self-doubt that may hinder your progress. When your thoughts, emotions, and self-perception are in alignment with your goal, you create a powerful internal environment for goal manifestation.

Techniques for Effective Goal Visualisation

a) Creating a Vision Board:

A vision board is a physical or digital collage that represents your goals and desires. Gather images, words, and symbols that resonate with your goals and arrange them on a board or create a digital collage. Display your vision board in a prominent place where you can see it daily. By regularly viewing your vision board, you reinforce your visualisation and keep your goals at the forefront of your mind.

b) Guided Visualisation Exercises:

Guided visualisation exercises involve following an audio recording or script that directs your imagination towards specific goal-oriented scenarios.. You can find guided visualisation resources online, in books, or through guided meditation apps.

c) Mental Rehearsal and Future Pacing:

Mental rehearsal involves visualising yourself engaging in the actions and experiences necessary to achieve your goals. By mentally projecting yourself into the future, you are experiencing the fulfilment of your goal as if it has already been achieved. By mentally rehearsing and future pacing, you create a sense of familiarity and comfort with the journey towards your goal.

d) Journaling and Scripting the Desired Outcome:

Writing down your goals and describing them in detail can be a powerful form of visualisation. Use a journal to write about your desired outcome as if it has already happened. Describe how achieving your goal looks, feels, and impacts your life.

e) Affirmations and Positive Self-Talk:

Affirmations are positive statements that affirm your desired outcome and align your thoughts with your goals. Create affirmations that are specific, present-tense, and emotionally resonant. Repeat your affirmations regularly, especially during visualisation practice, to reinforce positive beliefs and program your subconscious mind for success. Combine affirmations with positive self-talk throughout the day to maintain a positive mindset and align your thoughts with your goals.

My Experiment

- Visualisation became a routine practice for every aspect of my work.

- For every meeting I visualise myself on time at the meeting place and see the exact time of the meeting on my mobile phone. I have always been on time for all meetings.

- When I travel, I visualise myself along with my vehicle at the destination point and at the targeted arrival time. I have always arrived on time.

- If I visualise the type of food I would like to eat, most of the time that's the food that shows up on the dining table.

- I always visualise the outcome I am expecting from smaller to bigger tasks in my mind before starting.

Insights

- Visualisation is imagining what you want to achieve in the future as if it is true today.
- Repeatedly visualising the desired outcome will most likely manifest it in reality.
- For effective visualisation:
- Clearly define the desired outcome.
- Add specific details.
- Provide measurable milestones.

Action Steps

Example 1: Buying a car.

- Now I am driving my new blue-coloured BMW 5 series car, the tan-coloured leather seats are looking amazing.
- I am getting the fragrance of new leather. My life partner is sitting next to me .
- Wow ! I made it. Thanks to the universe.

Example 2: Buying a house.

- Now I am celebrating the house warming ceremony for my 5-bedroom villa with my family and friends. It is in a beautiful gated community. Today the date is 11th November 20_. Thanks to the universe, for such a beautiful house.

Write a few sentences on achieving your goal, the situation around you and your feelings. These sentences will help you in visualisation.

_____

_____

_____

_____

_____

_____

_____

The Power of Visualisation

WORKSHEET

12
Consistent-Persistence

Consistent persistence is a powerful tool that can help you achieve your dreams. Consistency and persistence are two important qualities that are essential for achieving success in any area of life.

Many people struggle with consistency and persistence when it comes to achieving their goals. However, those who can cultivate these qualities are often the ones who achieve the greatest success.

By cultivating these qualities, you'll be better equipped to overcome obstacles, stay motivated, and achieve long-term success. So, take the first step towards your goals and start developing consistent persistence.

Let's first define these two terms:

Consistency: The ability to do something the same way over a long period.

Persistence: The quality of continuing steadily despite problems or difficulties.

Consistency and persistence are often used together because they complement each other. Consistency helps to establish a routine and a sense of predictability, while persistence allows you to overcome setbacks and obstacles that inevitably arise when working towards your goals.

Without consistency, it's easy to get side-tracked and lose focus. Without persistence, it's easy to give up when faced with challenges. Together, these qualities create a powerful combination that can help you achieve your goals.

Some of the most Significant Benefits of being Consistent and Persistent are:

Increased Productivity: Consistency helps you to establish a routine and structure that can increase your productivity. When you do something regularly, you become more efficient at it, and you can complete tasks more quickly and effectively.

Improved Mental Health: Developing consistent routines can also have a positive impact on your mental health.

Greater Confidence: When you persist through challenges and setbacks, you develop greater confidence in your abilities. This confidence can help you to take on more ambitious goals and challenges in the future.

Enhanced Focus: Consistency helps to eliminate distractions and increase your ability to focus on the task at hand.

Long-term Success: By consistently working towards your goals and persisting through setbacks, you increase your chances of achieving long-term success.

Improved Time Management: Developing consistent routines and habits can help you to better manage your time.

Some of the common obstacles that can prevent you from being consistent and persistent and strategies for overcoming them are presented here.

Lack of Motivation: When you lack motivation, it's easy to give up on your goals or become distracted by other things. You can overcome this by rewarding yourself for your successes.

Postponing: When you postpone, you put off tasks and goals, making it difficult to make progress. You can overcome this by breaking tasks into smaller, more manageable pieces and setting deadlines for completing them.

Fear of Failure: When you are afraid of failing, you may be hesitant to take risks or try new things. Failure is not the end of the road, but rather an opportunity to learn and grow. You become more resilient and persistent in the face of challenges.

Lack of Accountability: When you are not held accountable for your actions, you may be more likely to give up on your goals. To overcome this you can find an accountability partner or join a group of like-minded individuals who share your goals.

Some Practical Strategies for Developing Consistency and Persistence:

Set Clear Goals: The first step in developing consistency and persistence is to set clear goals. This involves identifying what you want to achieve and breaking it down into specific, measurable, and achievable steps. Having clear goals gives you a roadmap to follow and helps you stay on track.

Establish Routines: Consistency requires establishing routines and sticking to them. This can involve creating a daily or weekly schedule and following it as closely as possible. By establishing routines, you can eliminate distractions and focus on your goals.

Track Progress: Tracking your progress is an important strategy for developing consistency and persistence. This involves regularly reviewing your progress towards your goals and making adjustments as needed. Tracking progress can also help you stay motivated and celebrate your successes.

My Experiment

- I have been maintaining consistency in raising early by 5 am for the last 15 years.
- Using Affirmations and Visualisation are almost a daily practice.
- I prepare a weekly schedule consistently and work accordingly.
- I am consistent in doing physical activity 5 days a week.
- I have been persistent in maintaining my core values even during low points in my life.

Insights

- Consistency is the ability to do something the same way over a long period of time.
- Persistence is the quality of continuing steadily despite problems or difficulties.
- Consistency helps you become more efficient.
- Consistency helps you complete tasks more quickly and effectively.

13
The Power of Scheduling

Do you often feel like there aren't enough hours in the day to get everything done? Do you struggle to balance your work, family, and personal life? The solution to this problem may be simpler than you think: **Scheduling.**

Scheduling is the process of planning and organising your time to achieve specific goals or tasks. It can take many forms, from a daily to-do list to a weekly calendar to a long-term project plan. The key is to find a scheduling method that works for you and helps you prioritise your time and energy.

Scheduling can help you reduce stress and anxiety by providing a sense of structure and control over your day. When you have a plan in place, you know what you need to do and when you have to do, which can help you stay focused and productive. Scheduling can help you achieve your goals by breaking them down into manageable tasks and ensuring that you're consistently working towards them.

Scheduling can help you in achieving a better balance in your life. By allocating time for work, family, hobbies, and other activities, you can ensure that you're making time for the things that matter most to you.

Types of Scheduling Methods

There are many different types of scheduling methods, and the right one for you will depend on your personal preferences, goals, and lifestyle. Some of the most common scheduling methods are:

Daily to-do list: Write down the tasks you need to accomplish, and cross them off as you complete them.

Weekly calendar: Use a calendar to block off time for specific tasks or appointments, such as work meetings, family time, exercise, and hobbies.

Long-term project plan: If you're working on a big project, such as writing a book or planning a wedding, a long-term project plan can help you stay on track. Break the project down into smaller tasks, and schedule each task on a calendar or to-do list. This can help you see the big picture and ensure that you're making progress towards your goal.

Time blocking: Time blocking is a technique where you block off specific times of day for certain activities. For example, you might block off 8am-10am for email and administrative tasks, 10am-12pm for creative work, and 1pm-3pm for meetings. This can help you stay focused and productive by reducing distractions and ensuring that you're making time for the things that matter most.

Prioritisation matrix: Create a grid with four quadrants: urgent and important, important but not urgent, urgent but not important, and not urgent or important. Then, place each task in the appropriate quadrant based on its priority. This can help you focus on the most important tasks.

	Urgent	**Not Urgent**
Importance	**Do:** Tasks with deadlines or consequences.	**Schedule:** Tasks with unclear deadlines that contribute to long-term success.
Not importance	**Delegate:** Tasks that must get done but don't require your specific skill set.	**Delete:** Distractions and unnecessary tasks.

The key to successful scheduling is to find a method that works for you and to stick with it. The goal of scheduling is to help you achieve your goals and live your best life, so don't be afraid to make adjustments as needed.

Tips For Effective Scheduling

Start with your priorities: When you're scheduling your time, start by identifying your priorities. What are the most important things in your life? What goals do you want to achieve? Once you know your priorities, you can schedule your time accordingly.

Be realistic: Don't try to cram too much into your day, or you'll end up feeling overwhelmed and stressed. Instead, be honest with yourself about how much you can realistically accomplish in a given day or week, and schedule your time accordingly.

Build in breaks: Schedule time for breaks, such as a walk outside or a meditation session, to ensure that you're taking care of yourself and avoiding burnout.

Be flexible: Life is unpredictable, and sometimes you need to adjust your schedule to accommodate unexpected events or changes in priorities. Be open to change and willing to adjust your schedule as needed to maintain a sense of balance and control in your life.

Avoid multitasking: When you try to do too many things at once, you're not able to focus fully on any one task, which can lead to mistakes and reduced productivity. Instead, focus on one task at a time, and give it your full attention.

Use technology to your advantage: There are many scheduling apps and tools available that can help you stay organised and on track. Find a tool that works for you, whether it's a calendar app, a to-do list app, or a project management tool, and use it to help you stay focused and productive.

Review and adjust: Finally, it's important to regularly review your schedule and make adjustments as needed. Check-in with yourself regularly to see if you're making progress towards your goals, and adjust your schedule as needed to ensure that you're on track.

My Experiment

- I schedule my action steps related to all my goals.
- I use a weekly calendar for my scheduling. Each Sunday I will prepare the schedule for the upcoming week. This really helps me focus on the right things and get them done.

Insights

- Scheduling is the process of planning and organising your time to achieve specific goals or tasks.
- Scheduling can help you stay focused and productive.
- The goal of scheduling is to help you achieve your goals and live your best life.

Action Steps

- Prepare a schedule for all your goals.

Typical Weekly Schedule

	Monday	Tuesday	Wednesday	Thursday	Friday	Saturday	Sunday
6.00 am							
7.00 am							
8.00 am							
9.00 am							
10.00 am							
11.00 am							
12.00 pm							
1.00 pm							
2.00 pm							
3.00 pm							
4.00 pm							
5.00 pm							
6.00 pm							

14
The Art of Giving

Giving is a powerful act that can have profound effects on your physical, emotional, and spiritual well-being. From a spiritual perspective, giving is often viewed as an expression of generosity, gratitude, and service to others. It is seen as a way to cultivate virtues such as compassion, kindness, and selflessness, and to contribute to the greater good of society.

However, science also supports the benefits of giving, providing evidence that giving can help to reduce stress, improve your mood, increase social connection, improve physical health, and potentially increase longevity.

By engaging in acts of kindness and generosity, you release hormones such as oxytocin, which can counteract the effects of stress hormones like cortisol and experience a sense of satisfaction and joy that can boost your mood and make you feel good about yourself.

Furthermore, when you give within the context of social relationships, such as volunteering with others or donating to a charity, you can strengthen your social ties and reduce feelings of loneliness and isolation.

Giving can have positive health benefits, such as lower blood pressure and reduced risk of cardiovascular disease. Ultimately, giving is a fundamental human act that can benefit both yourself and those around you.

Whether you give out of a sense of spirituality, a desire to help others, or a recognition of the benefits that giving can bring, the act of giving is a powerful expression of your humanity and a way to contribute to the greater good of society. So let us all cultivate a spirit of generosity, kindness, and compassion, and give freely to those in need.

"You make a living by what you get, but you make a life by what you give" the purpose of human life is to serve others. You are energy and the same energy is flowing through others, which means, you are serving your own self.

When you are helping others, you are bound to get back the help, though in a different form which you may not recognise. This is how the cosmic laws work. You are the giver and receiver on both sides. Understand this and cultivate giving in whatever form you wish. But give for your own benefit.

My Experiment

- As part of giving I am sharing my knowledge by writing this book.

- I built a 26000 sq. ft. Sri Prasanna Venkateswaraswamy temple on a 2 Acres land. This serves lakhs of people at Medchal, Hyderabad. I also built a Shirdi Sai temple at Kompalli, Hyderabad, Telangana. Temples serves as a belief and energy centres.

- I am one of the managing trustees in a non-profit organisation-SMILES TRUST, which takes care of 55 senior citizens and 28 underprivileged girl children.

- I am supporting some students for their higher education.

Insights

- Giving can benefit both yourself and those around you.

- Giving is a powerful expression of your humanity.

- The purpose of life is to serve others.

- You are energy and everyone is energy. Serving others means serving your own self.

- Give without expectation. You will always receive what you give, although it may be in a different form.

Action Steps

- Write here your proposed acts of giving.

15
Gratitude

Gratitude is a fundamental human emotion that has the remarkable ability to positively influence our lives. It goes beyond a simple "thank you" and delves into a profound state of appreciation for the people, experiences, and blessings in our lives.

When you cultivate gratitude, you shift your focus from what you lack to what you have, and in doing so, you open yourself up to a wealth of benefits that enrich your physical, mental, and emotional well-being.

Understanding Gratitude

Gratitude can be described as the heartfelt acknowledgement of the kindness, support, and goodness received from others or even from life itself. It is not merely a polite response to favour but a deeper appreciation of the interconnectedness of human experiences. Gratitude encourages you to recognize the efforts of others, the beauty of the world, and the positive aspects of your own life. It enables you to see the glass as half full instead of half empty, fostering a more optimistic outlook.

The Power of Gratitude

Gratitude has a profound impact on your mental health. When you regularly engage in the practices of gratitude such as keeping a gratitude journal or expressing thanks to others, you experience a greater sense of happiness and contentment.

When you express gratitude to others, you validate their actions and efforts, strengthening the bond between you. It creates a positive feedback loop where acts of kindness and appreciation are reciprocated, leading to more supportive and loving connections with family, friends, and colleagues.

Cultivating Gratitude

Cultivating gratitude in your life requires consistent effort and practice. Some effective ways to incorporate gratitude into your daily routine are:

Gratitude Journaling: Maintaining a gratitude journal can be a transformative practice. Each day, take a few minutes to write down three things you are grateful for and say thank you. This exercise helps shift your mindset towards appreciation and reminds you of the positive aspects of your life.

Expressing Gratitude to Others: Take the time to express your gratitude to the people who have made a positive impact in your life. Whether through a heartfelt thank-you note, a phone call, or a simple act of kindness, showing appreciation strengthens your relationships and spreads positivity.

Expressing gratitude to Health: When you are grateful for your health you will maintain your present health as well you can improve every function of your entire body. Say thank you to all your body parts.

Expressing gratitude to Money: Feel grateful and say thank you for the money you have now and received in the past, your money will increase in the future. The more you are grateful the more you receive.

Expressing gratitude to Food: Food and water are the greatest blessings given by the nature to us. Say thank you before you eat or drink; as a gratitude for the food and water.

Mindful Awareness: Practice mindfulness by being fully present and attuned to the world around you. Observe the small joys and beauty in everyday moments, whether it's the warmth of the sun on your skin, the laughter of loved ones, or the beauty of nature. Say thank you.

As you incorporate gratitude into your daily life, you not only positively impact yourself but also inspire a ripple effect of kindness and appreciation in the world around you. Be grateful, and share the gratitude with others to create a brighter and more harmonious world.

My Experiment

I daily say statements of gratitude to myself and feel thankful to the universe for giving me:

- Healthy and perfect body.
- Positive thoughts always.
- Spiritual knowledge.
- Perfect life partner.
- Healthy children with the right attitude.
- Beautiful house.
- Beautiful office.
- Luxury cars.
- Perfect team to deliver my goals.
- Supporting staff and drivers.
- Customers and investors.
- Friends and well-wishers.
- Profitable businesses.
- Positive business associates.

Insights

- Gratitude is saying thank you for what you are grateful for, with a deeper feeling.

- By cultivating gratitude, you shift your focus from what you lack to what you have.

- Gratitude strengthens relationships.

- Expressing gratitude for your present health will continue to improve your health.

- The more you are grateful for the money you have, the more you will receive.

- Say thank you before you eat or drink.

Action Steps

- Write down ten things you are grateful for and write why you are grateful for each one.

Example: I am really grateful to have What? because Why?

- Each one read from your list in your mind and say thank you, thank you, thank you and feel the gratitude.
- Write down three close relationships you are grateful for the say thank you.

Example :

Thank you_____for being a perfect life partner and taking care of each and every need of mine. Thank you. Thank you.

_____
_____
_____
_____
_____
_____
_____
_____
_____
_____
_____
_____

U R A Creator

16
Living with Non-Attachment

Attachment is a deeply ingrained aspect of human experience. You often form attachments to people, possessions, ideas, and outcomes, seeking security, pleasure, and identity. Attachment can also lead to suffering, as it binds you to expectations and creates resistance to change.

Everyone and everything in the world is in a constant state of flow. Nothing remains fixed or unchanging. By embracing the reality of impermanence, you can loosen your grip on attachments and find freedom from the struggles and disappointments that arise when you resist the natural flow of life.

Practising Non-Attachment

The practice of non-attachment requires mindful awareness and intentional effort.

Various practices and techniques that can help you cultivate non-attachment are:

Mindfulness Meditation: Through meditation, you develop the ability to observe your thoughts, emotions, and sensations without becoming attached or identified with them. By cultivating a non-judgmental awareness of the present moment, you create space between yourself and your experiences.

Letting Go of Expectations: You often hold onto rigid ideas about how things should be, how others should behave, or how events should unfold. By consciously letting go of expectations, you open yourself to the possibilities of the present moment and release the attachments that bind you.

Detaching from Outcomes: Instead of fixating on achieving a particular outcome, you learn to appreciate and engage fully in the present moment. By letting go of attachment to outcomes, you free yourself from the anxiety and disappointment that arise when things don't go as planned.

Cultivating Gratitude: Recognizing and appreciating the abundance in your life, you shift your focus from what is lacking to what is already present. Gratitude allows you to detach from the constant desire for more and invites you to fully embrace and enjoy the present moment. Gratitude helps you realise that true fulfilment comes from within rather than external circumstances.

Letting go of Control: Life is inherently uncertain and uncontrollable. By consciously letting go of the need for control, you release yourself from the grip of attachment.

Non-Attachment in Relationships: By letting go of possessiveness, expectations, and the need for the other person to fulfil your desires, you create space for authentic connection and growth.

Embracing the Present Moment: Recognise that everything in life is subject to change, you fully immerse yourself in the present moment. By letting go of attachments to the past or future, you can experience a deep sense of presence and appreciation for the here and now. The present moment is where life unfolds, and when you are anchored in it, you can enjoy its beauty, richness, and possibilities.

Expansion of Consciousness: You transcend the narrow perspective of the self and open yourself up to the interconnectedness of all beings and the greater web of existence. Non-attachment enables you to tap into your inherent wisdom and experience a profound sense of oneness with the universe.

Overcoming Obstacles to Non-Attachment

Attachment to Identity: You often derive a sense of self-worth and security from your roles, achievements, and labels. However, this attachment can limit your growth and prevent you from experiencing true freedom. Overcoming this obstacle requires cultivating self-awareness and recognizing that your identity is not fixed but fluid. By loosening your grip on rigid identities, you open yourself up to new possibilities and a deeper understanding of your true nature.

Fear of Loss: You fear losing loved ones, possessions, or your sense of control. This fear can keep you stuck to patterns of clinging and resistance. To overcome this obstacle, you must cultivate trust in the natural flow of life and embrace the impermanence of all things.

Desire and Craving: You constantly seek pleasure, validation, and external sources of happiness. However, these desires can keep you trapped in a cycle of grasping and dissatisfaction. Overcoming this obstacle requires cultivating mindfulness and developing a deep understanding of the transient nature of pleasure. By redirecting your focus from external desires to inner contentment, you can liberate yourself from the chains of attachment.

Conditioning: You are often conditioned to believe that certain possessions, relationships, or achievements will bring you happiness and fulfilment. These conditioned beliefs can be deeply ingrained and challenging to overcome. To address this obstacle, you must engage in self-inquiry and critically examine your beliefs and values. By questioning societal conditioning and aligning with your authentic truth, you can free yourself from attachments that do not serve your highest good.

Resisting Change: Change is an inevitable part of life, and resisting it only leads to suffering. To overcome this obstacle, you must cultivate acceptance and develop a willingness to embrace change. By practising mindfulness you can flow with the currents of life and find freedom in embracing the unknown.

Lack of Awareness: You may go through life on autopilot, unaware of your attachments and their impact on your well-being. Developing mindfulness and cultivating present-moment awareness is key to overcoming this obstacle. By paying attention to your thoughts, emotions, and behaviours, you can identify attachments as they arise and consciously choose to let them go. Awareness allows you to break free from the unconscious patterns that keep you attached and empowers you to make conscious choices aligned with non-attachment.

My Experiment

- I focus on the attainment of my goals. If I am attached to the end results; somewhere I have to compromise. But if I let go attachment and work towards the end goals I have seen the many fold benefits.

- I work with people so closely but simultaneously I am detached.

- I respect human emotions more than materials. I always keep myself detached from material things like vehicles, electronic items and objects.

- I don't get emotionally attached in any situation.

- I am not attached to the habits, schedules and even food. I keep myself flexible.

- Sometimes I work very intensely to get a project. But for if any reason, I don't win a bid in seconds, I will let that go and focus my energies on something else.

- If something doesn't happen, I say to myself that some other great thing is waiting and I move on.

- Internally I am free from all relationships and responsibilities, I always focus on what I want to experience but I am not attached to the outcome.

- I am non-attached due to my awareness. I always keep an eye on my thoughts and if needed I change them and move on.

- I am not attached to company positions, nor to being the head at family.

- Living with non-attachment is a practice. Once you master it, you enjoy your wealth and relationships thoroughly.

Insights

- Intentional effort is required to live with non-attachment.

- With non-attachment to the end results, you free yourself from anxiety and disappointment.

- Non-attachment enables you to experience a profound sense of oneness with the universe.

WORKSHEET

17

Living in the Present Moment

Many of us carry the weight of our past experiences or anxieties about the future. We are constantly pulled between regrets and memories of the past, fears and uncertainties about what lies ahead.

The past is merely a collection of memories, and the future is nothing more than a projection of your thoughts and imagination.

In reality, the only true moment you have is the present one. By recognizing the illusory nature of the past and future, you free yourself from unnecessary suffering and open yourself up to the richness of the now.

To live truly in the present moment, you must aware of your true nature. You often operate on autopilot, lost in your thoughts, worries, and distractions. By cultivating mindfulness and awareness, you can shift your attention from the incessant chatter of your mind to the vividness of the present.

Resistance to the present moment arises when you resist what is happening or look for things to be different. However, resistance only prolongs your suffering and disconnects you from the present reality. By embracing acceptance and surrender, you learn to flow with the unfolding of life,

Mindfulness is a state of conscious awareness that involves paying attention to the present moment with an attitude of curiosity, openness, and acceptance. It is about being fully engaged in what you are doing, experiencing, or feeling, without getting lost in thoughts about the past or worries about the future. Through mindfulness, you develop the ability to observe your thoughts, emotions, and sensations without judgement, creating space for insight and self-discovery.

Mindfulness Techniques and Exercises:

There are various techniques and exercises that can help you cultivate mindfulness and integrate them into your daily life. Here are a few practices to get started:

- ❖ **Breath Awareness:** Pay attention to your breath, observing the sensation of the breath entering and leaving your body. Whenever your mind wanders, gently bring your focus back to the breath.

- ❖ **Body Scan:** Scan your body from head to toe, noticing any sensations or areas of tension or relaxation. Allow your awareness to rest on each part of the body without judgment.

- ❖ **Mindful Eating:** Engage in your meals with full awareness. Notice the colours, textures, smells, and flavours of the food. Chew slowly and savour each bite, being fully present with the experience of eating.

- ❖ **Walking Meditation:** Take a mindful walk, paying attention to the sensations of each step—how your feet touch the ground, the movement of your body, and the surrounding environment. Stay present with each moment of the walking experience.

- ❖ **Loving-Kindness Meditation:** Cultivate feelings of love, kindness, and compassion towards yourself and others. Repeat phrases such as, "I am happy, I am healthy, I am at peace," extending these wishes to loved ones, acquaintances, and even challenging individuals.

- ❖ **Gratitude Practice:** Before going to bed, reflect on three things you are grateful for, from your day. Embrace the positive aspects of your present moment and cultivate an appreciation for the simple joys of life.

Integrating Stillness into Daily Life:

Beyond dedicated practices, integrating stillness into your daily life is essential for living in the present moment. Some ways to incorporate stillness into your routine include:

- Create a ritual; either in the morning or evening for a deep reflection and introspection.

- Carving out moments of silence throughout the day, such as during meal times or by taking gaps between the activities.

- Setting boundaries with technology and creating tech-free zones to allow for stillness and disconnection.

My Experiment

- I keep my full awareness on whatever work I am doing.

- In all interactions I listen with 100% attention. While listening I don't correlate with the existing data in my mind and also I don't think about what to say next while listening. I only listen.

- Whenever possible, I will keep a beautiful smile on my face. When we are smiling we are only in the present moment, we cannot be in the past or future. Now smile and check.

- I observe plants/trees and their leaves moving to keep myself in the present moment without any analysis.

- I observe birds and their actions without judging their next moments or co-relating with other birds. Just watching with full awareness.

- I observe the movement of ants. Just watching. No interpretations. These are some of my practises for staying in the present moment.

- In my office meetings I just focus on one subject with one team without any distractions from other staff or from my mobile phone. I am just living in that moment.

- When I am with my family I will give undivided attention so that I am not missing them. Even if I spend a small amount of time, it is quality time which helps me connect well with all my family members. This is possible only when I am living in the present moment.

- When I am eating I engage myself with my food. I enjoy eating my food. I bless my food and I am thankful to the food for becoming part of me. Even if others are speaking I just focus internally on chewing my food.

- I watch movies just like a kid. I am 100% immersed. My phone goes on silent. I am not aware of what's happening next to me. I am just being in that moment.

- Because of living in the present moment I don't have time to stay in the past. I am always engaged with live actions.

Insights

- The only true moment you have is the present one.

- You must be aware of your true nature to live in the present moment.

- Living in the present moment is about being fully engaged in what you are doing, experiencing, or feeling ,without getting lost in thoughts about the past or about the future.

WORKSHEET

18

Meditation

Meditation is simply being in a state of pure delight-not engaged in any action, thought, or emotion. When all activity is paused, both physical and mental, you are left with "Just Being".

Thinking, concentrating, and contemplating are all forms of doing. When you can be without doing anything, even for a brief moment, and find yourself deeply relaxed at the centre of your being, that's meditation. Once you acquire this skill, you can stay in this state for as long as you wish. This is the first aspect of meditation-just being.

The second aspect involves carrying out tasks while staying in this meditative state, from small actions like brushing your teeth or showering to more complex ones. Meditation is not against action; it doesn't demand that you escape from life. It simply offers a new way to live. Your life proceeds with greater intensity, joy, clarity, creativity, and vision. You become an observer, watching things happen around you without being the one doing them.

You can engage in large or small tasks, but the key is not to lose your centre. Just being in the moment is blissful which brings immense joy and satisfaction that nothing else can compare to.

The spirit of meditation is a process of learning how to observe. A keen observation is meditation. It doesn't matter what you observe-it could be birds flying, a river flowing, waves on a beach, a sunset, ants moving around, or clouds. The essence of meditation lies in the quality of observation, the quality of being aware and alert.

Meditation is awareness. Anything you do with awareness becomes meditation. Listening to music or birds, or even your inner voice, can become a meditation if done with awareness. Simply put, anything done consciously and with awareness is a meditation that doesn't require a goal.

The process of awareness involves several steps:

1. Start by being aware of your body, which will become more relaxed.

2. Next, become aware of your thoughts. As you watch your thoughts, they gradually fall into a pattern.

3. Lastly, be aware of your feelings, emotions, and moods.

Once you are aware of these three aspects, they unify and function together perfectly. Then, the ultimate awareness occurs spontaneously. This is the awakened state where you come to know blissfulness. Blissfulness is the goal, and awareness is the path towards it.

Meditation is essentially a practice that makes you aware of your real self. Real self isn't a creation of your own, You don't need to create it; you are born with it. When a person starts knowing his real self, he starts identifying himself as divine. He lives according to his inner truth, without societal fear.

Everyone is unique-search for your uniqueness.

Meditation helps to develop your intuition.

To meditate means to become a witness, to become aware of the external and internal things, and thoughts, happening right at a given moment. Meditation isn't a technique per se. Techniques can lead to Meditation. Eventually, techniques become redundant-they are merely actions. There are various methods to practise meditation until you reach a point where you can attain the state of meditation just by not doing anything-just being there, and it happens.

Body Posture:

Body posture is crucial in meditation because your mind shouldn't be stressed about the posture. You can sit in the lotus position, half lotus, cross-legged, on a chair, or even lie down with a straight spine and relaxed arms. Your eyes can be lightly closed or tightly shut, whatever makes you comfortable.

Your mouth, jaws, and teeth should be completely relaxed, and your head should be naturally balanced without any tilt.

The key to meditation is to be in a comfortable posture that lets you forget about your body.

The Three Essentials For Meditation Are:

1. **A relaxed state of mind:** There should be no internal struggle in your mind. If your mind isn't controlled, you won't achieve concentration.

2. **Awareness:** You should be conscious of whatever is happening in your mind. This should be a deeply relaxed awareness without any interruption.

3. **Observation:** Watch your mind without any judgement or calculation.

When you start meditating, it's best to do it regularly for a short period, such as 10 to 20 minutes.

Here's a simple exercise: Sit in a quiet place and concentrate on your breath for a relaxed state of mind.

1. Become aware of your body. Concentrate on each part of the body from head to toe.

2. Once you are in this state, consciously be aware of your thoughts. Observe the thought flow without any judgement or conclusions. Just be the watcher of your thoughts.

3. Practise small mindful activities, as simple as just sitting and observing moving cars or leaves while being aware of your body and thoughts.

4. Practise one mindful activity a day with full awareness.

5. Once you can maintain this state for a long time, try to practise multiple activities with full awareness.

Meditation Techniques:

1. **Mindfulness Meditation:** This technique involves bringing your attention to the present moment and focusing on your breath or a specific sensation in your body. When you notice your mind wandering, simply acknowledge the distraction and bring your attention back to your breath or sensation. This type of meditation can help you develop greater self-awareness and focus, and can also reduce stress and anxiety.

2. **Transcendental Meditation:** This technique involves repeating a mantra, which can be any word or phrase that has a calming effect on your mind. You sit with your eyes closed and repeat the mantra silently to yourself, allowing your mind to settle into a state of deep relaxation. This type of meditation can be particularly helpful for reducing stress and improving overall well-being.

3. **Loving-Kindness Meditation:** This technique involves directing positive thoughts and feelings towards yourself and others. You can start by visualizing someone you care about and repeating phrases like "May you be happy, may you be healthy, may you be safe, may you be at peace." Then, you can extend those same positive feelings towards other people in your life, and eventually towards all living

beings. This type of meditation can help cultivate feelings of compassion, empathy, and connectedness.

4. **Body Scan Meditation:** This technique involves focusing on each part of your body, one at a time, and observing any sensations or tension that you may feel. You start at the top of your head and slowly work your way down, paying attention to any areas of discomfort or tightness. This type of meditation can help you develop greater body awareness and release tension in your muscles.

5. **Visualisation Meditation:** This technique involves creating a mental image of a peaceful, relaxing scene or environment, and focusing on it in order to reduce stress and anxiety. For Example You might imagine yourself in a peaceful forest or by the ocean, and focus on the sights, sounds, and sensations of that environment. This type of meditation can help reduce anxiety and promote relaxation.

6. **Chakra Meditation:** This technique involves focusing on the energy centers of the body, known as chakras.

There are seven chakras, each associated with different physical and emotional qualities. By focusing on each chakra and using Visualisation or breathing techniques, you can promote balance and healing throughout your body and mind.

Henceforth, there are many different types of meditation and each one can offer its own unique benefits. It's worth experimenting with different techniques to find the ones that resonate with you and help you achieve your meditation goals.

Typical Daily Meditation :

1. The Circle of Compassion–Self-compassion fills you from within, allowing you to radiate love to others.

    a) Feel a sense of love within you, encompassing your entire body.

    b) Expand this circle of love to your home, city, country, planet, and the entire universe.

    c) Visualize the world and universe.

    d) Feel the love coming back to you.

2. Gratitude –

    a) Express gratitude for five things in your personal life.

    b) Do the same for your professional life.

    c) And for yourself.

3. Forgiveness–You can forgive everything and anything. Pardoning frees you.

4. Envisioning the Future –

    a) Imagine a giant TV screen 6–9 feet in front of you.

b) Think about 1-3 important goals for the next three years and put these images on your mental screen.

c) Imagine with all your senses-What do you see, hear, touch, taste, and feel ?

5. Your Perfect Day -

   a) Think about the segments of your day.

   b) Visualize each segment unfolding perfectly.

   c) Make a 10-second mental declaration to have an incredible day.

6. The Blessing -

   a) Imagine a beam of light coming down and feel the warmth emanating throughout your body down to your toes.

   b) Thank the universe.

My Experiment

- I daily meditate for 25-30 minutes in morning hours.
- Most of the time, I live in the present moment that itself is a meditation.

Insights

- Meditation is simply being in a state of pure delight.
- Finding yourself deeply relaxed at the centre of your being is meditation.
- Being in the moment is blissful, which brings immense joy and satisfaction.
- A keen observation of your thoughts or actions with being aware and alert is meditation.
- Practising meditation makes you aware of your real self.
- Everyone is unique. Search for your uniqueness.

19
The Importance of Yoga

Thanks to modern science, you now understand that you are made of atoms and that you are surrounded by an infinite amount of energy that is continually changing.

The great seers and sages of ancient India created the science of yoga through divine inspiration and contemplative visions. Yoga offers knowledge on issues pertaining to your destiny. Yoga provides the tools for the experiential understanding of the Divine self.

It tells you that you are in charge of determining your own future and level of happiness. Gaining inner knowledge and realising your true, eternal self are the main goals of human life.

Yoga represents union. Yoga teaches you to live in harmony and unity while showing compassion and deference to every living thing in the natural environment. Yoga encompasses more than just a regimen of physical activities. It includes the body, mind, awareness, and soul are in that order. Every person can learn about his inner nature and the true meaning of life through yoga.

Yoga helps you realise your inter connectedness with all other living things and the entirety of creation. Humans most potent force is their capacity to think.

Yoga is defined as a scientific system that combines moral guidelines for behaviour with physical postures, breathing, concentration, and meditation exercises.

Only humans have the cognitive capacity to comprehend "what is energy". Only humans have the capacity to recognise their divinity and realise that they are not the ones who act. The cosmos alone is the doer, it is the universe that acts through us.

The ultimate expression of consciousness, which is the conscious connection of the individual soul with the divine self, is found in the continuing evolution and enlightenment of awareness.

The soul cannot be defined or explained. Space is the most comparable example. You cannot cut, burn, or destroy space. Space is always space; it can be separated into "individual" spheres that can be formed by placing fences or walls along its perimeter, but as soon as these barriers are taken down, the undivided, united space re-emerges.

The body, mind, intellect, temperament, attributes, and experiences gathered as the "person" indicate the boundaries for self for a while, just as walls divide space. The energy does not change, although the body and the individual do. Your true self is eternal, unborn, and unchangeable.

Yoga philosophy offers solutions to fundamental queries like "Who am I ?"

Ask yourself: Are you a body? The brain? Your attributes?

Thoughts? Feelings?

Or do you have another identity?

You become more aware of the subtler facets of your being as you look deeper and deeper, all the way down to the level of the elements.

Finally, you acknowledge that you yourself are.

Sat-Truth

Chit-Consciousness Ananda-Bliss

The everlasting, limitless, and unchanging soul is the essence of your divine selves, and this is what you refer to as 'Sat-Chit-Ananda'. The soul is the only authentic reality you possess. Every other thing is untrue. The conscious observer of everything that occurs, the soul is also known as "Chaitanya" and is the knower of the past, present, and future.

The primary goal of life is to achieve Sat-Chit-Ananda, also known as the Ultimate Bliss.

Through yoga, you can awaken this slumbering power within you and use it for your personal well-being as well as the benefit of the entire planet.

Actions and their Results

Everything in the universe is consciousness; it is the fundamental force that vibrates within each atom.

Only humans have complete freedom from prejudice and the ability to choose their activities. Only humans have the capacity to consciously shape and alter their lives.

Since you are "I" consciousness-oriented, you carry responsibility for your own actions. Hence choose your actions consciously as per the desired outcome. Every action you perform will eventually return to you in the same form that it left you. This is the cosmic law of action.

You produce the effect of action in 4 ways:

- Through thoughts
- Through words
- Through actions that you perform yourself.
- Through actions that others do under your instructions.

After death, the physical body stays on this earth, and decays. The constituent elements in the body separate from one another and return to their original source as atoms. The mind continues to exist and we find ourselves once more as a spiritual, body-less person in the astral world. All of our thoughts, information, and memories are stored in the atomic mind.

After we die, we lose one thing: our "Kriya shakti," or willpower. We are only capable of performing good or harmful things in our physical bodies. We are powerless to accomplish anything when we pass away. Our material things, titles, and positions on earth are now worthless.

Whatever degree of the universe you achieve is solely a result of your actions or past deeds. Everything that happens to you is the "fruit" of your history because you sow the seeds of your future through your deeds.

Positive thoughts and behaviours improve happiness and give your future possibilities, but negative thoughts and behaviours increase the effects of tragedy on your destiny.

If our fate was predetermined long before our physical bodies existed, we would essentially be "puppets" being pulled along by an unavoidable fate. Is that happening to us? Not at all. We have the power to influence and change the course of events.

Even though the occurrences in our destiny are the result of our prior deeds and are being guided by them. However, we have the choice to turn away or with the least impact by how we are acting right now.

You are in a position to alter the direction of your destiny or future because you have control over the actions you take today, but only if you act appropriately at the appropriate time.

Relief From Past Deeds: Through constructive deeds, righteous thoughts, prayers, and meditation, you are able to remove the effects of your past deeds from this life and eventually change your future.

Positive Actions: Kindness, mercy, assistance, selfless service, praying, meditating, and using mantras and affirmations, among other practices-produce a positive, healing energy that enlightens and cleanses your own energy and radiates all around you.

Negative Actions: Such as those motivated by resentment, hatred, envy, attachment, passion, greed, or fanaticism create negative energy, and vibration around you.

"The whole world exists in your mind."

Every concept, feeling, and thinking exists in its own realm. You can only take charge of your future by learning to regulate your mind. The best way to master the mind is to cultivate positive thoughts and traits.

Nadis-Energy Channels

The awareness known as Energy flows through energy pathways called Nadis. The 72,000 Nadis, or subtle and flawless networks, that make up the human body distribute this life force throughout the entire body. The Nadis correspond to the nervous system on a physical level, but they also have an impact on the astral and spiritual realms of existence. You are healthy and generally pleased when all the Nadis are working properly. However, almost all of us have some sort of bodily or psychological issue, which suggests that some of the Nadis need to be balanced since some of them are malfunctioning.

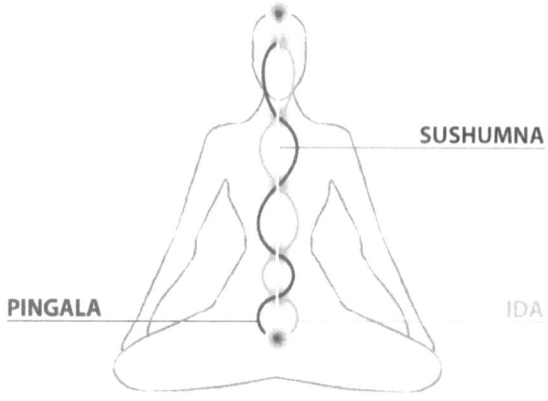

Three Nadis, IDA, PINGALA, and SUSHUMNA, are particularly significant.

IDA, which stands for the moon principle, emerges on the left side of the body.

The right side of the body is where PINGALA, which represents the solar principle, emerges.

SUSHUMNA, which represents consciousness, runs through the spinal cord's central channel.

PINGALA, IDA, and SUSHUMNA all have physical counterparts in the sympathetic nervous system, parasympathetic nervous system, and central nervous system, respectively.

Through the breath, you may energise and harmonise the Nadis. When doing Pranayama, breathing through the left nostril opens the Ida Nadi. The Ida Nadi has cooling, calming, and revitalising properties similar to the moon's silvery light. However, inhaling through the right nostril affects the Pingala Nadi, which has a warming and energising effect.

Ida and Pingala start in the brain roughly where the pituitary gland is located. Ida affects the right hemisphere of the brain, whereas Pingala affects the left. Both Nadis move from one side of the body to the other in a snake-like motion to maintain equilibrium. The central Nadi, Sushumna, is likewise met at the sites where they intersect. Very potent energy centres known as CHAKRAS occur in the locations where the strength and radiance of the sun, moon, and Sushumna combine with the fortifying impact of the Sushumna.

Only one stream of consciousness—the Sushumna Nadi's spiritual energy flows when the three primary Nadis come together. This Nadi is also where the energy passes through when in Samadhi and extended meditation. Thoughts, feelings, concerns, and other mental activities are constantly changing as long as the Sushumna is dormant. However, as soon as the Sushumna starts to flow, the mind's waves stop, and we can "bathe" in the joy of divine consciousness.

Chakras in the Human Body

Chakras are an integral part of Yogic science, a profound system of knowledge and practice that originated in ancient India. The term "chakra" comes from Sanskrit, meaning "wheel" or "disc," symbolizing the energetic vortexes within the human body. Yogic philosophy proposes that these chakras are centers of spiritual power and vital energy, influencing physical, emotional, and mental well-being.

The Concept of Chakras

According to Yogic science, the human body contains seven primary chakras, aligned along the spinal column, from the base of the spine to the crown of the head. Each chakra is associated with specific qualities and attributes, and they are believed to be interconnected, forming an intricate network that regulates the flow of energy throughout the body.

7 Chakras in Human Body

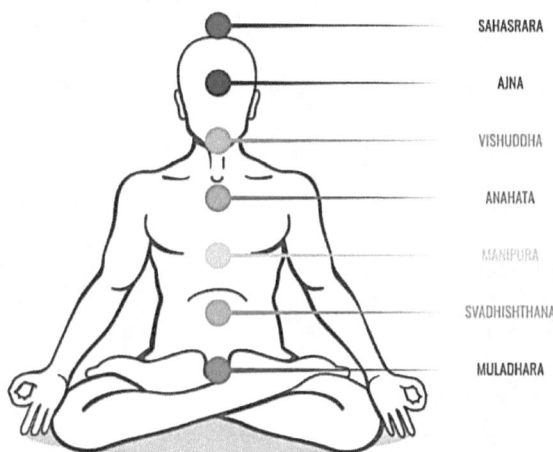

a) **Muladhara (Root Chakra):** Located at the base of the spine, the Muladhara chakra is associated with the element of Earth and represents our foundation and sense of security. It is the center of physical vitality and basic survival instincts. Balancing this chakra promotes a sense of stability, grounding, and connection to the physical world.

b) **Swadhishthana (Sacral Chakra):** Positioned just below the navel, the Swadhishthana chakra is connected to the element of Water and governs our emotions, creativity, and sensuality. A balanced sacral chakra fosters healthy relationships, emotional expression, and artistic endeavours.

c) **Manipura (Solar Plexus Chakra):** Situated in the upper abdomen, the Manipura chakra is linked to the element of Fire and represents personal power, confidence, and self-esteem. When in harmony, this chakra supports assertiveness and a strong sense of purpose.

d) **Anahata (Heart Chakra):** Located in the center of the chest, the Anahata chakra is associated with the element of Air and embodies love, compassion, and interconnectedness. A balanced heart chakra fosters empathy, forgiveness, and harmonious relationships.

e) **Vishuddhi (Throat Chakra):** Positioned at the throat region, the Vishuddhi chakra is connected to the element of Ether and is related to communication, self-expression, and authentic voice. Keeping this chakra balanced promotes clear and truthful communication.

f) **Ajna (Third Eye Chakra):** Situated between the eyebrows, the Ajna chakra is associated with intuition, inner wisdom, and spiritual insight. It governs the mind and allows for heightened perception and spiritual growth.

g) **Sahasrara (Crown Chakra):** Located at the crown of the head, the Sahasrara chakra represents the highest level of consciousness and spiritual connection. It is associated with pure awareness, enlightenment, and transcendent experiences.

Balancing and Aligning the Chakras

The proper functioning of chakras is crucial for maintaining physical, emotional, and mental well-being.

Yogic practices, such as asanas (physical postures), pranayama (breath control), meditation, and mantra chanting, are essential tools to balance and align the chakras.

a) **Asanas:** Each chakra is associated with specific yoga poses that stimulate the corresponding energy center. For example, grounding poses like Mountain Pose (Tadasana) help balance the Muladhara chakra, while Cobra Pose (Bhujangasana) activates the Anahata chakra.

b) **Pranayama:** Controlled breathing techniques influence the flow of prana within the body, clearing energy blockages and harmonizing the chakras. Alternate Nostril Breathing (Nadi Shodhana) is an effective pranayama practice to balance the entire energy system.

c) **Meditation:** Chakra meditation involves focusing on each chakra, visualizing its associated colour and symbol, and allowing the energy to flow freely. This helps in identifying imbalances and promoting overall harmony.

d) **Mantra Chanting:** Chanting specific mantras, such as "Om" or the mantra associated with each chakra, activates and purifies the respective energy centers.

Chakras and Holistic Health

When the chakras are balanced and aligned, they facilitate the free flow of energy, leading to physical, emotional, and mental well-being.

a) **Physical Health:** A balanced Muladhara chakra enhances physical vitality, while a harmonious Manipura chakra supports digestive health and metabolism. A clear and open throat chakra (Vishuddhi) aids in better communication and thyroid function.

b) **Emotional Health:** Anahata, the heart chakra, is central to emotional well-being. A balanced heart chakra allows for the expression of love, compassion, and empathy while releasing repressed emotions.

c) **Mental Health:** The Ajna chakra plays a vital role in mental clarity and intuition. A balanced Third Eye chakra promotes enhanced perception, focus, and decision-making abilities.

d) **Spiritual Growth:** Sahasrara, the crown chakra, is the gateway to higher consciousness and spiritual enlightenment. Awakening this chakra is associated with profound spiritual experiences and self-realization.

My Experiment

- I practice yoga 3 to 4 times a week. Doing asanans and pranayama help me stay focused.

Insights

- Yoga provides the tools for the experiential understanding of the Divine Self.
- You can learn about your inner nature and the true meaning of life through yoga.
- Your true self is eternal, unborn and unchangeable.
- The soul is the only authentic reality you possess. Every other thing is untrue.
- The primary goal of human life is to achieve the state of ultimate bliss.
- You can consciously shape and alter your life.
- You can only take charge of your future by learning to regulate your mind.
- Chakras in the human body are centers of spiritual power and vital energy, influencing your physical, emotional and mental well-being.

WORKSHEET

20

You Are Perfect

You are a perfect being at all times. You are absolutely flawless. You are more than simply a physical being, you are awareness, consciousness, and vast energy. You can build, move, think, act, and even destroy.

Consciousness is the energy that gives life in different forms. The entire universe is teeming with life and is pulsing with vibrant energy. There is nothing that is not life; life is everything. You have this amazing human experience as a spiritual being, you have been given this amazing, great, astounding consciousness as a gift.

You may appear to make mistakes or fail, but you are always a perfect spiritual being. You may believe you are not quite competent, not entirely attractive, or that you lack other qualities. You remain a perfect being, nonetheless.

For a deeper understanding of this concept, consider electricity a form of ideal energy, it occasionally runs on a malfunctioning device. Electricity still maintains its perfection; it is essentially a pure form of energy. Similarly, even though you are a perfect, radiant being, your physical body may appear as not functioning effectively. But you are, nonetheless, a perfect being.

You must understand that your physical body does not entirely define who you are. A flawless spiritual entity is what you are. Get used to the notion that you are perfect.

As soon as your brain starts working, you start creating an idea of who and what you thought yourself to be. All your life experiences have been shaped based on "Who you think you are."

Your true perfection gets covered by layers of false images, and misconceptions. But you can change that to surface the real perfection.

The Power of Your Imagination

Your imagination and subconscious mind are strong instruments. They respond to an imagined event that is quite similar to a real encounter.

Your imagination can transform you when you are in a relaxed condition, referred to as the alpha state. Our brain cycles at about 8-12 cycles per second while in the alpha state. The average rate of brain activity as we are going about our daily lives, thinking, problem-solving, and processing information functions at around 13 to 30 cycles per second, this is called the beta level. Sleep comes when our brain is operating at eight cycles per second and lower. At this point you are in the alpha state. You are also at the alpha level when you are just waking up and during the day when you are relaxed but aware of consciousness. At this stage, you are creative and more receptive to suggestions. Your imagination acts powerfully on your subconscious mind and is effective in producing desired results.

Allow your mind to roam freely in imagination. Don't hold back. Begin by seeing yourself the way you like to see yourself. If you would like to be slimmer or in top physical condition see yourself the way you wish. Remember your subconscious mind doesn't know the difference between imaginary experience and real experience. Both experiences are real to your subconscious mind.

Overwriting Your Old Self Image

You will enter into an alpha state and use your imagination to create a new image of yourself that will overwrite your current image in your subconscious mind of "who you think you are". Your new image is "who you want to be", once this is placed in the subconscious mind, "what you want" will naturally happen. It is equivalent to re-recording over a CD.

Your physical self, your career self, your social self, your student self, and all other selves that make you up will now be seen as perfect. You feel much better about yourself as you continue to expose your conscious mind to your subconscious perfect picture, and you will produce outcomes that are in harmony with your perfect image. One of the best ways to change who you are and attract the things you want is to become the person you want to be.

Believe in the universe. Everything and every event that occurs is the best thing that could possibly happen to you. You are a perfect being in a perfect universe, where everything occurs entirely for your own benefit. You should completely believe in this.

Read the next paragraph aloud, as though you have written it.

"This is my time to have the circumstances of my life the way I want them. The universe responds to me. I participate in directing and controlling the outcome of events in my life. I participate in creating the circumstances of my life, moment by moment. To change outward circumstances, I first make changes in myself. I am aware of, 'Who I am' at every moment. I am a pure bright spirit-a perfect being. I act with the knowledge that the universe only responds to what I want."

Repeat the following sentences in a whisper:

From now on,

- I have complete control of every circumstance.
- I will always be able to identify the precise course of action.
- I experience vigorous health.
- I possess the things I desire.
- My life is peaceful and harmonious.
- I experience amazing love and abundance.

- I claim all these things as my own from this moment onwards.

Know that whatever good you envision is now on its way to you and will be reaching you.

My Experiment

- I always feel I am perfect in every aspect and I am perfect.

Insights

- You are more than a physical being, you are awareness, consciousness and vast energy.

- All your life experiences have been shaped based on who you think you are.

- Your imagination acts powerfully on your subconscious mind and is effective in producing the desired results.

- You are a perfect being in a perfect universe, where everything occurs entirely for your own benefit.

- Say to yourself-I am a pure, bright spirit-a perfect being. I act with the knowledge that the universe responds to only what I want.

21

Living Daily

We don't know when we will end our human experience.

Let us live life to the fullest daily, so that we have no regrets.

It's all about how, we are managing our 16 hours of waking time effectively.

Divide your day into different segments and live to the fullest.

Based on the knowledge gained, you design your own typical day, to stay healthy, wealthy and joyful.

Example of a typical day :

1. Rising early-5 am

Once you rise, the first things to do are:

   a) Rub your hands and keep on your face and feel the energy.

   b) Doing little stretching

   c) Visualise your day

   d) Make your bed

- e) Do a few push-ups (or super brain yoga)-11 times
- f) Laugh, while looking at yourself in the mirror.
- g) Mindfully brush your teeth.

2. Doing Meditation: 20-30 minutes
3. Doing physical activities: 45-60 minutes

Walking / yoga / working out in Gym / Play badminton

4. Schedule your day-10 minutes
5. Visualisation: 15 minutes
   - a) Visualising the planned activities of the day with the desired outcome.
   - b) Visualise the end results of short-term and long-term goals
   - c) Read your affirmations on your well being
6. Taking shower and getting dressed: 20 minutes
   - a) Mindfully take a shower while placing your awareness on your hands
   - b) Get dressed with full awareness.
7. Breakfast: 15 minutes

   Eating healthy food with awareness.
8. Delivering your career responsibilities: 10 am-6 pm.

   Schedule these 8 hours as per your work requirements.

9. Working on self-awareness activities: 6 pm-7 pm
    a) Reading books
    b) Listening to podcasts
    c) Meditation
10. Spending time with children: 7pm-8pm
11. Family time: 8pm-9pm
12. Retiring from the day.

Universe Expects Me to Live Like

- I am the universe and My physical body is the universe.
- I am the awareness and I am placing my awareness where I wish.
- My thoughts become true and My body transforms it into action.
- My new self-talk is -
  a) I am creating my joyful life.
  b)
  c)
  d)
  e)
  f)
- My core values are -
  a) I respect every human being.
  b)
  c)
  d)
  e)
  f)

- My meaning for success is –

  _____

  _____

  _____

  _____

  _____

- My compelling life vision is :

  _____

  _____

  _____

  _____

  _____

- I know what I want. My intuition leads the way. My short-term goals are –

  a)

  b)

  c)

  d)

  e)

  f)

My long-term goals are-

a)

b)

c)

d)

e)

f)

- My commitment to my life is -

_____

_____

_____

_____

_____

- My new habits are
    a) Following a daily schedule.
    b)
    c)
    d)
    e)
    f)

- My affirmations are

    a) I attract all that I want and need into my life now.

    b)

    c)

    d)

    e)

    f)

    g)

    h)

    i)

    j)

- Imagination is more important than knowledge. I am daily imagining/visualising on –

    a)

    b)

    c)

    d)

    e)

    f)

- I am consistently pursuing my new goals and living with my new habits.
- I am preparing my weekly schedule and living accordingly.
- I have decided to give the following as part of giving-

    a)

    b)

    c)

- I am grateful to/for

    a)

    b)

    c)

    d)

- I am perfect in every aspect of my life. I will have everything but need nothing. I Love my self unconditionally.
- I have goals but I am not attached to the end results. I am enjoying the journey of achieving the goals.
- I am living in the present moment. My daily practices for perfection on this

    a)

    b)

    c)

- I am following my daily meditation schedule

  a) Morning 20 minutes: _ am to __am.

  b) Evening 15 minutes: _ pm to _ pm.

- My body is important to experience the purpose for which I came. I am taking care of it with daily yoga / physical activities..

- I am following the 16 hours daily schedule with flexibility to have a meaningful life.

Signature :   Date :

References and Further Reading

The Mind:

Dandapani (2022), The Power of Unwavering Focus, Penguin, pp 69-71, 152, 185, 189-193,

Joseph Murphy (2011), The Power of Your Subconscious Mind, Amazing Reads

Self-Talk:

Shad Helmstetter, (2017), What to Say When You Talk to Yourself, Pocket Books, pp 72-81, 115-128

The dream about your life:

John C. Maxwell (2016), 3 things successful people do, Nelson books, pp 35-39.

Setting your goals:

Mark Victor Hansen, Jack Canfield, Les Hewitt (2013), The Power of Focus, Vermilion, pp 66-88

Developing Habits :

Mark Victor Hansen, Jack Canfield, Les Hewitt (2013), The Power of Focus , Vermilion, pp 8-27

Meditation :

Osho (2004), Meditation,

Osho International Foundation.

The Importance of Yoga :

Paramhans Swami Maheshwarananda (2004), The Hidden Power in Humans, Ibera Verlag, pp 9, 21-23, 51, 52

You are Perfect :

Chris Prentiss (2010), Be Who You Want Have What You Want, Wisdom tree, pp 52, 54

www.ingramcontent.com/pod-product-compliance
Lightning Source LLC
LaVergne TN
LVHW041705070526
838199LV00045B/1215